THE JOURNEY
from
MANUSCRIPT
to
PRINT

Kirk House Publishers

THE JOURNEY
from
MANUSCRIPT
to
PRINT

A GUIDE TO PUBLISHING YOUR BOOK

ANN AUBITZ

First Printing: April 2024
First Edition

Paper Back: 978-1-959681-18-2
eBook: 978-1-959681-19-9
Hardcover: 978-1-959681-20-5
LCCN: 2024933887

Interior and cover design by Ann Aubitz
Author headshot by Amy Zellmer

Published by Kirk House Publishers
1250 E 115th Street
Burnsville, MN 55337
kirkhousepublishers.com
612-781-2815

CONTENTS

INTRODUCTION

The long road from manuscript to printed book can be daunting for aspiring authors. You have poured your heart and soul into your masterpiece, but how do you actually get it published? As a publisher, I have seen many writers struggle to navigate the publishing process. This unknown territory is often the biggest hurdle between completing a manuscript and holding your published book in your hands.

The process is complex, with many steps and players involved. It's difficult to know where to start or who to turn to for advice. Most authors only publish one or two books in their lifetime, so they are learning as they go. Meanwhile, publishers see hundreds of books through each phase of development. This disparity of knowledge puts writers at a disadvantage.

It is frustrating and disheartening to realize how much work remains after your manuscript is "done." Editing, proofreading, formatting, cover design, printing, distribution—the list goes on. You thought the hard part was behind you, but the road stretches endlessly ahead.

The good news is you don't have to figure it all out alone. As a publisher, I can offer guidance through each stage, drawing on decades of experience. I want to demystify the process for you, so you can bring your book to market successfully. I organized the book with brief chapters for easy reference, but not necessarily in chronological order, since you are often doing multiple tasks simultaneously. You also will notice several steps that seem repeated, and it may be the case since you use the same information for multiple steps.

Your manuscript deserves to become the professional, polished book you have always envisioned. Let's get started!

THE STATE OF BOOK PUBLISHING

T he state of book publishing in the world today is a complex and ever-evolving industry. Here are a few key points to consider:

Digital Transformation: With the rise of e-books and audiobooks, the publishing industry has experienced a significant digital transformation. More readers are embracing digital formats, leading to an increase in digital sales.

Self-Publishing: Self-publishing has become more accessible and popular in recent years. Authors can now bypass traditional publishing houses and choose to self-publish their books, thanks to platforms like Amazon Kindle Direct Publishing and Smashwords.

Diversity and Inclusion: There has been a growing emphasis on diverse and inclusive voices in publishing. The industry is making efforts to publish more books that reflect a wider range of cultures, races, ethnicities, and perspectives.

Consolidation: The industry has seen consolidation among major publishing houses over the years. This consolidation might affect the diversity of voices and reduce the number of opportunities for new and emerging authors.

Challenges: The book publishing industry faces challenges such as piracy, declining bookstores, and increasing competition from other entertainment mediums. However, the continued love for physical books and the emergence of new distribution channels like online bookstores and subscription services offer potential opportunities.

Overall, book publishing is a dynamic industry that continues to adapt and navigate the changing landscape. The rise of digital platforms, self-publishing, and increasing diversity are some of the notable trends shaping the industry today.

PART 1
THE WRITING PROCESS

Note from the author: I am a member of an amazing women writers' group. The membership consists of authors who have not yet published anything, women who have been working on their memoirs for fifteen years, and women who have published and have gone on to meet the President of the United States or were interviewed by Oprah.

The breath of their experience is wide, but they all have one thing in common—the lack of time to write. That is the biggest issue that most writers have in our much too busy world. In this section, you will read tips on finding the perfect writing place for you, different methods for time management, and ideas to spark creativity.

I wrote this book with different levels of writers in mind. I tried to think about all the writers I know and give ideas for different stages of a writing career so you can use the book as a resource and refer to it when needed.

CHAPTER 1
The Elusive Search for Writing Time

"I can't wait to get started on my book!" says every aspiring author ever. Yet despite our best intentions, actually sitting down to write often remains an elusive goal amidst the busyness of everyday life.

Finding time to write can indeed be one of the biggest struggles for authors. Whether you're a new writer working on your first manuscript or a seasoned author with books under your belt, carving out a consistent time and space for your craft presents an ongoing challenge.

The aim of this chapter is to explore actionable techniques that can help authors create the time and headspace needed to make consistent progress on their writing projects. Though the demands of our time are many, with some planning, focus, and dedication, writers can adopt strategies that make their literary aspirations an achieved reality.

The Busyness Epidemic

Today's world seems increasingly busy and hectic. Between work, family commitments, household chores, and other obligations, many people find themselves constantly on the go with little free time. For writers trying to carve out time for creative projects like writing a book, this busyness presents a major hurdle.

Unlike past eras, modern life often demands people multitask and fill each moment with productivity and action. Quiet contemplation or creative work gets pushed aside by seemingly more urgent to-dos. Constant digital distractions like email and social media fracture people's attention spans, making it hard to focus on writing. The 9-to-5 no longer confines work either; many employees feel pressure to be available and working at all hours. Writers struggle to protect time for the deep thinking, research, planning, and sustained focus that writing a book requires.

With so many responsibilities and commitments competing for their time, authors often end up deprioritizing their passion projects. But writing regularly and carving out undistracted time remains essential to producing a book. Authors who want their writing to flourish amidst the daily whirlwind must get strategic in how they manage their schedule. Certain techniques and lifestyle choices can help authors protect and optimize their writing time.

CHAPTER 2
Find a Place to Write

The best place to write can vary from person to person, as it depends on individual preferences and needs. However, here are some ideas for places that are often conducive to writing:

Home office or dedicated writing space: Having a designated area in your home specifically for writing can help create a focused and productive atmosphere. Set up a desk or a comfortable writing nook where you can write without distraction.

Coffee shops or cafes: Many writers find the ambient noise and the buzz of a coffee shop or cafe to be inspiring and stimulating. The casual atmosphere can help get the creative juices flowing. Find a spot with a comfortable chair and a good Wi-Fi connection if needed.

Libraries or bookstores: These places often provide a quiet and contemplative environment that encourages concentration. Surrounding yourself with books and the energy of others engaged in reading or writing can enhance your focus and creativity.

Parks or outdoor spaces: If you find inspiration in nature or enjoy fresh air while writing, consider going to a park, garden, or any outdoor space. Being in a serene environment can help clear your mind and spark creativity.

Co-working spaces: These shared workspaces provide a productive atmosphere, often with amenities like quiet rooms, comfortable seating, and a professional environment. They can be helpful if you need a dedicated space away from home distractions.

Museums or art galleries: The displays of art and exhibitions at museums or art galleries can be a source of inspiration. Some of these establishments offer designated writing spaces or cafes where you can write surrounded by creativity.

Public transportation: If you have a long commute on public transportation, it can be an opportunity to write. Use that time to jot down ideas, work on outlines, or even start writing drafts. Just find a comfortable seat and have a notebook or a laptop handy.

Retreat or getaway locations: Consider going on a writing retreat or finding a quiet getaway spot where you can immerse yourself in your writing without distractions. Whether it's a cabin in the wilderness or a rented space in a picturesque location, a change of scenery can be invigorating.

The best place to write is wherever you feel most comfortable, focused, and inspired. Experiment with various locations and find what works best for you. What matters most is creating an environment that supports your writing process and allows you to tap into your creative flow.

CHAPTER 3
Time Blocking

Time blocking is a time management method that involves setting aside specific blocks of time dedicated solely to writing. This allows authors to protect parts of their schedule and prevent other obligations from encroaching on their writing time.

To implement time blocking:

Identify when you have the most energy and focus for writing. For many, this is the first thing in the morning.

Block off chunks of time during your optimal writing periods in your calendar app. Start with 30 or 60-minute blocks and increase as you build momentum.

Consider these blocks as appointments that you cannot move or interrupt except for true emergencies.

Eliminate distractions during the blocked periods by turning off phone notifications, closing email, and isolating yourself from interruptions.

Focus completely on writing during the allotted time blocks. Set a timer to keep yourself accountable.

Start small and be consistent. It's better to block 15-30 focused minutes daily than a two-hour block once a week.

Build up your blocked time as your stamina increases. But keep sessions short enough to maintain focus.

Vary locations to maximize fresh inspiration. Try writing from a cafe, library, or park for some blocks.

With consistency over time, time blocking can enable authors to carve out dedicated writing time even amidst the busiest schedules. The key is being intentional, focused, and protecting the blocked-out periods. This investment will pay dividends on completing a book.

CHAPTER 4
The Pomodoro Technique

The Pomodoro Technique is a time management method that uses a timer to break work into intervals, traditionally 25 minutes long, separated by short breaks. This method can help authors focus during writing sessions while also incorporating periodic breaks to recharge.

To use the Pomodoro Technique for writing:

- Choose a task, such as writing a section of your book. Set a 25-minute timer.
- Work on the task until the timer rings. Avoid distractions and stay focused.
- When the timer rings, take a short 3–5-minute break. Stretch, grab a drink, or take a walk.
- After the break, reset the timer for another 25-minute writing session.
- Complete 3-4 pomodoros. After your 3-4 focused sessions, take a longer break, from 15 to 30 minutes.
- Start the process over, beginning with step 1.

The timed sessions help writers focus intensely while the scheduled breaks ensure they don't burn out. This rhythm of concentrated spurts followed by relaxation allows authors to be productive while also caring for their mental wellbeing. With practice, the Pomodoro Technique can help authors establish a regular writing routine amidst the demands of their busy lives.

CHAPTER 5
Focusing on the Most Vital Priorities

In the busyness of life, it's easy to get distracted by less important tasks. Parkinson's Law states that work expands to fill the time available. By limiting writing time, authors can focus their efforts on the most vital writing priorities.

Some strategies for prioritizing writing include:

- Rank writing tasks by importance and urgency. Focus first on high-importance, high-urgency tasks.
- Schedule writing time on your calendar before other events and tasks. Treat it as immovable.
- Set daily or weekly word count goals to make progress.
- Limit distractions and avoid multitasking during writing time.
- Say no to nonessential tasks and obligations that eat up writing time.
- Wake up early to write when energy and focus are high.
- Use productivity methods like time blocking to dedicate set times for writing.
- Break large projects into smaller daily goals to make them more manageable.
- Reward yourself after meeting writing goals.

With focus and determination, authors can create time for their most important writing priorities, even within packed schedules. By learning to focus efforts on vital tasks, writers can make consistent progress.

CHAPTER 6
Writing in the Morning

Many authors (not all) have found that writing in the morning hours can be more productive than other times of the day. The morning offers a fresh start after a night's sleep, making it easier to focus without distractions from the rest of the day. It's helpful to get up early and develop a regular morning writing habit.

Here are some tips for creating a productive morning writing routine:

- Wake up at least one hour before you need to start writing. Use this time to exercise, meditate, or do other morning rituals so you're energized for writing.
- Avoid checking email, social media, or news first thing so you don't lose focus.
- Start by writing longhand in a journal if that helps generate ideas before going to the computer. Julia Cameron's Morning Pages technique advocates three pages of stream-of-consciousness writing every morning.
- Write for a set time period like 60-90 minutes instead of aiming for word count. Use a timer so you don't keep checking the clock.
- Have a dedicated writing space if possible, and all your supplies organized the night before.

- Reward yourself after your writing session with breakfast and a healthy morning routine before tackling the rest of the day's work.
- Consider pairing up with an accountability partner or writing group to stay motivated.

Developing a consistent morning writing habit takes commitment but can help authors protect time for their creative goals. Writing first thing in the morning can set the tone for a productive writing day.

CHAPTER 7
The Morning Pages

Julia Cameron's *The Artist's Way* introduced the concept of Morning Pages as a tool for unlocking creativity and making time to write. The idea is simple but powerful—write three pages of longhand, stream-of-consciousness writing, every morning.

To make Morning Pages a habit:

- Write morning pages by hand, not typing. Handwriting engages your mind differently.
- Write continuously for your three pages. Don't worry about grammar, spelling, editing, or even making sense. Just keep your pen moving.
- Date your Morning Pages each day. This helps track your progress.
- Write Morning Pages in a dedicated notebook you enjoy using. Having a special place for this writing makes it feel more ritualistic.
- Commit to practicing daily. Be patient through resistance at first to establish consistency.
- Morning Pages help authors in many ways.
- Drain negative thoughts, worries, and stuck energy, freeing mental space.

- Gain clarity, insight, and new ideas through stream-of-consciousness writing.
- Build writing stamina and overcome blank page anxiety through daily practice.
- Access your inner voice and find inspiration for authentic writing.
- Establish a contemplative writing ritual that nurtures creativity.

Remember that Morning Pages serve as a form of meditative writing to empty your thoughts onto paper. The practice helps clear mental space so you can focus on creative work. Cameron recommends writing Morning Pages first thing after waking, before reading, talking, or checking devices.

CHAPTER 8
Writing on Retreat

Taking an extended writing retreat can provide authors the focused time needed to make significant progress on a book project. By getting away from regular distractions and obligations, authors can immerse themselves in writing for days or weeks at a time.

When planning a writing retreat, it's important to choose a location that will be conducive to productivity. Ideally, it should be some place quiet and free from household responsibilities. Many writers opt to visit a rented cabin, hotel, or vacation rental for their retreat.

To make the most of the dedicated writing time, authors should arrive prepared with research completed and an outline mapped out. Retreat locations with Wi-Fi access allow for fact-checking and online research as needed. Writers should also plan to disconnect from email, social media, and other digital distractions during retreat writing blocks.

It's helpful to establish a structured daily writing routine for the retreat. This may involve writing for set hours each morning and afternoon, with breaks for meals, exercise, and relaxation in between. To avoid losing writing momentum, authors can schedule word count or page count goals for each retreat writing session.

Taking retreats regularly allows writers to make consistent progress on book projects. Scheduling follow-up retreats once initial drafts are complete also provides opportunities for intensive editing and rewriting sessions. With strategic planning, writing retreats enable authors to put their book projects front and center, despite their busy lifestyles.

CHAPTER 9
Forming a Writing Group

Writing is often a solitary endeavor, but coming together with others can fuel creativity, provide motivation, and garner feedback. For authors looking to finish a book, being part of a writing group could be the key to staying on track.

If you don't already belong to a writing group, consider joining or forming one in your area. Meet regularly, whether weekly or monthly, to discuss works-in-progress, hold each other accountable, and provide support. For the group to flourish, make sure all members are serious writers committed to the craft. Set guidelines upfront on logistics, critique methods, and confidentiality of shared works.

When forming a new writing group, start by asking writer friends if they'd be interested in joining. Reach out to writers you admire through social media or mutual connections. Local libraries, bookstores, writing centers, and Meetup groups are other places to find potential members. Ideally, aim for 4-8 engaged participants.

To facilitate rich discussions, have members bring printed copies of a few pages to share. Take turns reading aloud and then provide thoughtful feedback on what's working well and potential areas for improvement. Make sure criticism is constructive, not hurtful. Also discuss issues members face in the writing process and collectively brainstorm solutions. While the group's input will prove invaluable, the author should decide what final changes to make.

A successful writing group becomes a trusted community as friendships develop. Set the intention to support one another through the highs and lows of the writing life. We should share notes of congratulations when we achieve milestones and empathize when challenges arise. Help hold each other accountable by checking on progress and goals. Works written with the encouragement of a writing group can make authors feel less alone in their endeavors.

CHAPTER 10
Ideas to Spark Creativity

Authors can find imaginative ideas for creating fresh stories in several ways. Here are some strategies to spark creativity and generate fresh ideas:

Read: Reading is one of the most effective ways to gain inspiration and trigger creative ideas. Explore different genres, fiction and non-fiction, classics, and contemporary works. Pay attention to how authors craft their stories, develop characters, and build interesting plots. Exposing yourself to diverse narratives can help you discover new ideas and perspectives.

Observe the world around you: You can find inspiration in everyday life. Pay attention to the people, places, and events happening around you. Engage your senses and observe the details. Curiosity and observation can help you uncover unique story angles or interesting character traits.

Ask "What if?": Prompt your imagination by asking "What if?" questions. What if the laws of gravity suddenly stopped working? What if animals could communicate with humans? Explore different scenarios and let your mind wander. This technique can lead to unexpected and imaginative story ideas.

Embrace personal experiences: Draw from your own life experiences for inspiration. Reflect on memorable moments, challenges, or unique encounters. These personal insights can be the foundation for authentic and relatable stories.

Explore history and mythology: Delve into historical events, myths, and legends. Adapt them or use them as a springboard to create something new. You can reimagine ancient tales, give them a modern twist, or explore lesser-known historical figures or events.

Experiment with writing exercises and prompts: Engage in writing exercises or use writing prompts to challenge your imagination. Set a timer and write continuously for a specific period, explore different genres, or write from a random first line. These exercises can help break through creative blocks and generate unexpected story ideas.

Brainstorm with others: Collaborate with fellow writers or creative individuals to brainstorm ideas. Sharing thoughts and bouncing ideas off each other can spark new concepts and perspectives. Consider joining writing groups or taking part in workshops where you can engage with like-minded individuals.

Engage in free writing: Allow yourself to write freely without judgment or a specific goal in mind. Set a timer and write whatever comes to mind. Let your thoughts flow without restricting yourself. Free writing can often uncover hidden ideas and themes.

Keep a journal or idea notebook: Maintain a journal or notebook where you record random ideas, observations, or snippets of conversations that catch your attention. This can serve as a repository of potential story ideas that you can revisit when you're looking for inspiration.

Remember, in finding imaginative ideas, there are no strict rules. Each writer has their unique creative process. Experiment with different techniques, find what works for you, and nurture your imagination by constantly seeking new experiences and keeping an open mind.

CHAPTER 11
Overcoming Writer's Block

Writer's block can frustrate and discouraging, but there are strategies to overcome it. Here are some techniques to help you get past writer's block:

Take a break: Sometimes, stepping away from your work can provide a fresh perspective. Engage in activities that relax or inspire you, such as going for a walk, listening to music, or reading a book. Allow your mind to rest and recharge.

Set realistic goals: Break down your writing tasks into manageable chunks. Set specific, achievable goals for each writing session. This can help ease the pressure and make the process feel more manageable.

Try freewriting or stream-of-consciousness writing: Write without worrying about grammar, structure, or coherence. Let your thoughts flow freely onto the page. This technique can help bypass the internal editor and allow new ideas to emerge.

Change your environment: Sometimes, a change of scenery can stimulate creativity. Write in a different location, such as a coffee shop, library, or park. Surround yourself with unfamiliar sights, sounds, and smells to stimulate your senses.

Experiment with different writing exercises: Engage in writing exercises or prompt to jump-start your creativity. Write a scene from a unique character's perspective, explore unrelated topics, or try a new writing style. These exercises can help loosen up your creativity and break through blocks.

Seek inspiration from other sources: Read books, watch movies, or explore art forms outside of writing that inspire you. Engaging with different forms of creativity can spark new ideas and perspectives.

Eliminate distractions: Create an environment free from distractions. Turn off notifications on your phone, close unnecessary browser tabs, and find a quiet space where you can focus solely on your writing.

Break down the task into smaller steps: Sometimes, writer's block can stem from feeling overwhelmed by the enormity of the writing task. Break it down into smaller, more achievable steps. Focus on one paragraph, a dialogue exchange, or a character's backstory. By tackling smaller portions, you may find it easier to get back into the flow.

Write through the block: Don't wait for the inspiration to strike. Sit down and write, even if you don't feel motivated. Start with a simple task, such as describing a setting or writing a character's physical appearance. Often, getting started is the hardest part, and momentum will build as you write.

Seek support and feedback: Share your work-in-progress with trusted friends, writing groups, or writing communities. Getting feedback and support from fellow writers can provide new insights and encouragement.

Remember, writer's block is a common challenge, and it's normal to experience it at times. Be patient with yourself and persevere through the process. With time and persistence, you can overcome writer's block and continue making progress in your writing journey.

CHAPTER 12
Write What you Know

Mark Twain's Timeless Advice or is it an Outdated Mantra? The famous American author Mark Twain coined the phrase "Write what you know" in the late 19th or early 20th century. Twain, whose real name was Samuel Clemens, lived from 1835 to 1910 and is best known for his classic novels about life in the 1800s along the Mississippi River, including "The Adventures of Tom Sawyer" and "Adventures of Huckleberry Finn."

The Appeal of Writing What You Know

It is easy to understand why Twain's advice to "write what you know" resonates with many writers. Writing about your own firsthand experiences, knowledge, and interests can feel natural and effortless in a way that writing about unfamiliar topics does not. When you are writing about something you know intimately, the words flow freely. There is no struggle to understand concepts or research details. You can vividly describe events, places, emotions, and more by relying on your memory and expertise.

Writing from personal experience also lends an air of authenticity that can be difficult to recreate when writing about a foreign subject. The specifics seem real and genuine because they are—

you lived them. Readers may find it easier to immerse themselves in a story or relate to your perspective when they sense you have first-hand experience. The passion and conviction you have for subjects close to you often comes through in your writing as well.

Overall, drawing from your life experiences, knowledge base, and interests can feel natural and uncomplicated compared to stepping into uncharted territory. Mark Twain captured that sentiment with his widely quoted advice.

Potential Downside of Only Writing What you Know

While the familiarity of writing about your own experiences can make the writing process easier, adhering too strictly to the "write what you know" maxim can have some potential downsides as well.

It can limit the variety of stories and perspectives you can share. If a writer only focuses on their own direct experiences, they may miss opportunities to tell stories about people, places, time periods, or topics outside of their own background. Some of literature's most beloved works came from authors imaginatively transporting themselves into lives very different from their own.

It can restrict a writer's creativity. Strictly following real-life events or one's own knowledge may hamper a writer's ability to invent stories, characters, and fictional worlds that capture a reader's imagination. Some level of imagination is crucial for fiction writing.

Audiences may crave fresh insights. Readers often appreciate discovering new perspectives, ideas, and information that takes them outside their own realm of knowledge. If a writer remains too tethered to their own experiences, they may not provide the sense of discovery readers seek. Expanding beyond the familiar requires research and immersion into new topics.

It focuses on writing about the past versus the future. Our own experiences are by definition in the past. To envision possible futures, invent speculative scenarios, or imagine technologies and worlds that do not exist yet require moving beyond the limits of current knowledge. Science fiction and innovative genres illustrate the power of imagination unbound by the known.

So, while writing what you know provides a solid starting point, expanding beyond those boundaries can open up new worlds of possibility for writers and readers alike. The most impactful writers balance their own experiences with exploration of the unfamiliar.

Expanding Beyond Your Experiences

While writing about your own experiences can provide you with easy content, sticking solely to what you know can limit your writing. Expanding beyond your own life requires using research, imagination, and empathy to explore new topics and perspectives.

Doing research allows you to learn about topics and backgrounds outside of your direct knowledge. Immersing yourself in research materials gives you the foundation to write authoritatively on subjects you didn't previously know much about. Whether reading books and articles, interviewing experts, or traveling to gain first-hand experiences, research is key for widening your lens.

Using your imagination also enables you to write beyond your own life. You can envision fictional worlds, characters, and scenarios. Your imagination allows you to transcend your circumstances and write creative stories that feel authentic, even if you haven't directly experienced them yourself. Practicing imaginative exercises like character sketches or scenario planning can flex your creative muscles.

Cultivating empathy, or the ability to understand and share the feelings of others, is another important skill. Putting yourself in someone else's shoes through thoughtful consideration of their experiences, struggles, and emotions can help you write diverse, inclusive characters and situations. Striving for empathy provides insight into the human condition that aids writing about topics beyond your personal range.

Rather than limiting your writing solely to your own experiences, use research, imagination, and empathy to expand the possibilities. This provides broader topics to engage readers while allowing you to grow as a writer. With an open mindset and some diligent work, you can write insightfully about many subjects, not just what you already know.

Balancing Writing What You Know and Exploring New Topics

Twain's advice to "write what you know" contains wisdom, but one should not follow it dogmatically. The most impactful writing often comes from balancing writing about familiar experiences with exploring new topics and ideas.

Writers can thoughtfully combine personal knowledge with fresh concepts using a few strategies.

Research extensively before writing about an unfamiliar topic. Immerse yourself in books, articles, films, and primary sources to become knowledgeable. Take detailed notes and keep track of sources.

Start with what you know, then expand outward. If you have a personal experience related to the topic, describe it briefly to ground the piece in a familiar context. Then broaden the scope.

Find a novel angle or perspective on a familiar topic. Examine it through a different cultural lens or spotlight an overlooked aspect. Make fresh connections between ideas.

Co-create work with an expert in another field to merge your strengths. Collaborate on a piece, combining both your expertise.

Focus on universal human experiences and themes. Our shared hopes, struggles, and emotions connect us all. These can provide a foundation, even when writing about unfamiliar subjects.

Learn by doing. You don't have to be an expert to write. The act of creating a draft will expand your knowledge and reveal gaps for further research.

The best writing draws from both intimate firsthand experiences and new information gleaned through curiosity and study. With care not to present inaccurate information, writers can thoughtfully blend the known and unknown.

CHAPTER 13
Write your Book!

Writing a book can be an exciting and rewarding process. Here are some steps to help you get started:

Define your idea: Start by identifying the idea or concept that you want to explore in your book, consider the genre, themes, and audience for your story.

Plan and outline: Create a rough outline of your book, including the main plot points, characters, and settings. This will serve as a roadmap for your writing and help you stay organized.

Develop your characters: create well-rounded and believable characters. Think about their backstories, personalities, motivations, and how they will interact with each other within the story.

Set writing goals: Establish a writing routine and set goals for yourself. Whether it's a certain number of words or hours per day, having goals can help you stay motivated and make consistent progress in your book.

Start writing the first draft: Begin writing the first draft of your book. Don't worry too much about perfection at this stage; just focus on getting your ideas on paper. Let your creativity flow and embrace the fact that you can revise and edit later.

Revise and edit: Once you have completed the first draft, take a break and come back to it with fresh eyes. Read your manuscript and revise for plot holes, inconsistencies, and areas that need improvement. Edit for clarity, grammar, and style.

Seek feedback: Share your work with trusted beta readers, writing groups, or professional editors. Getting feedback can provide you with valuable insights and help you make further improvements to your book.

Polish and complete: Make the revisions based on the feedback you received. Pay attention to the overall flow, pacing, and character development. Consider hiring a professional editor for a final round of editing before publishing.

Remember, writing a book takes time, effort, and dedication. Embrace the creative process, be open to learning and improving, and stay committed to bringing your story to life.

Part 2

YOUR TARGET MARKET

Note from the author: I mention the word "target" ninety-four times in this book regarding the target market or the target audience for your book. I know it is repetitive, but it is important, probably one of the most important things when writing and marketing a book.

Most times my client's eyes gloss over when I talk about this subject, and most times they have already finished their manuscript. Some think about the person they are writing the book for, but truthfully, some authors only give their target market consideration when marketing.

I like to think of my reader as I am writing my manuscript. I treat them as a character. I answer basic questions about the person I am writing for, like demographics, but I go farther than that. I find an image online and treat that person as a reader of my book. I answer character development questions about my reader that go beyond just demographics.

CHAPTER 14
Defining Your Target Market

When writing a book, understanding your target audience clearly is crucial. Knowing who you are writing for will not only help you shape your content, but also determine your marketing and promotional strategies. In this section, we will discuss the importance of defining your audience and provide some tips on how to do it effectively.

Why is defining your target audience important?

Focused Content: Identifying your potential readers allows you to tailor your content specifically to their needs, interests, and preferences. This ensures that your book will resonate with your readers and provide them with valuable insights or entertainment.

Efficient Marketing: Knowing your audience aids in creating effective marketing strategies. You can reach out to the platforms or communities where your audience is most active, increasing the chances of attracting their attention and generating sales.

Connect with readers: Understanding your target audience enables you to establish an emotional connection with your readers. By addressing their problems or desires, you can create an interesting narrative that resonates with them on a deeper level.

Tips for defining your target audience:

Research: Conduct thorough market research to identify the demographics, interests, and buying habits of your potential readers. Look for patterns that align with your book's subject or genre.

Create Personas: Develop fictional characters or personas that represent your ideal readers. Consider their age, gender, occupation, interests, and motivations. This exercise helps you visualize and understand your audience on a more personal level.

Analyze Competitors: Study the books or authors who have a similar audience. Analyze their marketing strategies, content, and engagement with readers. This will provide valuable insights into your audience's preferences and expectations.

Engage with readers: Interact with your potential readers through social media, online communities, or book clubs. This direct engagement allows you to gather feedback, understand their needs, and build relationships with your audience.

Test and Iterate: Once you have defined your target audience, test your assumptions by sharing sample chapters or excerpts, organizing beta reader groups, or conducting surveys. Use the feedback received to refine your content and marketing strategies.

Stay Open-Minded: While defining your audience is crucial, it's essential to remain flexible and open-minded to discovering new segments or niches within your target market. Be willing to pivot your strategies if new opportunities arise.

In conclusion, defining your target audience is a fundamental step in successfully promoting and connecting with readers for your book. By understanding their desires, needs, and preferences, you can create content that resonates with them and develop effective marketing strategies. Remember, the more specific and detailed your understanding of your target audience is, the higher your chances of achieving success with your book.

Revisiting Your Target Audience

Once your book is complete and you market, it can be helpful to re-evaluate who your target audience is. Even if you spent time at the start defining your ideal reader, your actual audience may end up differing from what you initially envisioned.

There are several reasons revisiting your audience's definition is important:

Your ideas about the book's audience may have changed or evolved through the writing process. As you wrote more, you may have realized that the book appeals to a different demographic than originally thought.

Marketing the book exposes it to new potential readers. You may find unexpected audiences gravitating towards your book or that certain groups you targeted are not engaging as hoped.

Reader feedback provides insight into who finds your book valuable. Looking at reviews and comments can reveal if your intended audience resonates with the book or if other groups respond more strongly.

Your own perceptions of the topic may have shifted after completing the manuscript. Re-evaluating through fresh eyes allows you to reconsider the audience with your new knowledge and perspective.

To assess if your current audience definition is effective, look at metrics like sales figures, website traffic, email open rates, and social media engagement. See if the groups you have targeted are converting into readers and fans of your work.

You can also directly ask your current readers' questions to better understand them. Send out surveys asking how they found the book, why it appealed to them, what else they like to read, and basic demographic questions. Look for patterns to determine if your intended audience matches your actual audience.

Being open to revising your target audience can optimize your marketing efforts. Ensure you are spending time and money to reach the audiences most likely to appreciate and share your book. An accurate target audience model is essential for effective book marketing.

Adapting Your Market

As you market your book, you may find that your original target audience definition needs some tweaking. Initial assumptions about who your book would appeal to may prove to be off base after you dig into promotion. The people you thought would be interested in the book might not respond to your marketing messages. Or you may discover an unexpected audience that resonates strongly with your book. This presents an opportunity to adapt and expand your marketing approach.

Being flexible and pivoting to reach the people who most want to read your book is key. Here are some ways to adapt your marketing strategy:

Monitor analytics: Pay attention to which marketing channels drive the most traffic and engagement. Double down on promoting in the places that work.

Run A/B tests: Try different covers, book descriptions, or ad copy and see which convert better. Experiment with new marketing messages.

Ask for feedback. Survey or interview readers to get insights into what drew them to your book.

Follow engagement: See which topics or angles get the most shares or discussion. Incorporate those into your marketing.

Expand into new communities: Look for adjacent audiences that your content would also appeal to. Research where they are most active online or offline.

Consider a re-position: Repackage your book for a different audience by changing the title, cover, etc.

Partner with influencers: Work with people who have a strong pull with your revised target market. Collaborate on giveaways or content.

Adjust social media: Change your profile descriptions and bios to better speak to your real audience. Use relevant hashtags.

Update marketing materials: Refine your website copy, Amazon listing, press kit, etc. to match your new strategic focus.

Being nimble and pivoting in your marketing approach takes effort but helps ensure you reach the audience most likely to appreciate and share your book. Listen, analyze, and keep adapting.

CHAPTER 15
Study Online Behavior

Online behavior refers to the actions and conduct of individuals or groups when they are engaging with the internet and online platforms. It encompasses how people interact, communicate, and behave online, including their choices, preferences, and responses to various stimuli. Understanding online behavior is crucial for effective marketing, especially for promoting and selling a book.

To market your book effectively online, here are some key things you need to know:

You need to identify who your book is meant for and understand the demographic characteristics, interests, and preferences of your target audience. This knowledge will help you tailor your marketing messages and strategies to resonate with your specific audience.

Establish an online presence: Create a website or a landing page dedicated to your book where potential readers can find information about it. You can also consider creating social media profiles on platforms that are popular among your target audience.

Content marketing: Produce relevant and valuable content related to your book's topic and share it through a blog, social media posts, or guest articles on other websites. This will help establish you as an authority in your field and attract potential readers.

Engage with your audience: Respond to comments, messages, and reviews from your readers. Engage in conversations, address their queries, and show appreciation for their feedback. Building relationships with your audience can lead to word-of-mouth recommendations and increased visibility for your book.

Use online advertising: Consider using online advertising platforms like Google Ads, social media ads, or book promotion websites to reach a wider audience. Target your ads based on your book's genre, keywords, or demographics to increase the chances of reaching potential readers.

Seek book reviews and endorsements: Positive reviews and endorsements can be powerful tools for promoting your book. Reach out to influencers, bloggers, or reputable review websites in your book's genre and request reviews or endorsements. These testimonials can help build credibility and attract more readers.

By understanding online behavior and implementing effective marketing strategies, you can increase the visibility of your book and connect with potential readers in the digital landscape.

CHAPTER 16
Consider Demographics

When writing a book, it's important to consider the demographics of your potential readers. Understanding who your readers are will help you tailor your writing style, language, and even the themes and topics you choose to write about. Here are some of the key demographics you should gather information on:

Age: Knowing the age range of your readers can help you write in a style and tone that's appropriate for them. For example, if your book targets young adults, consider including more action and romance.

Gender: Understanding the gender of your readers can also be helpful in crafting your book. For example, if you're writing a book about a teenage girl's coming-of-age experience, focus on themes that apply to young women.

Geographic location: Knowing where your readers can be important in deciding what topics and themes would apply to them. For example, if you're writing a book set in a specific city or country, include details that are unique to that location.

Education level: Understanding the education level of your readers can help you choose the language to use in your writing. If your readers have a high level of education, use more advanced vocabulary and complex sentence structures.

Interests: Knowing the interests and hobbies of your readers can also help you tailor your writing to their preferences. For example, if you're writing a book about sports, include anecdotes or stories that apply to sports enthusiasts.

By gathering this information about your readers, you can create a targeted approach to your writing that will help you connect with your intended audience and make your book more successful. Keep in mind that these demographics are just a starting point, and you should always be open to feedback and adjust your writing accordingly.

CHAPTER 17
Realize Not Everyone Will Buy Your Book

I t may sound harsh, but once you get it in your head that not everyone is going to buy your book, you can focus on who will buy your book. Recognizing that not everyone will buy your book is an important mindset shift for authors. Instead of trying to appeal to everyone, it's more effective to focus on identifying and understanding the specific group of readers who are most likely to be interested in and purchase your book. By focusing on this audience, you can tailor your marketing efforts and messaging to reach and engage them effectively.

Here are a few steps to help you identify and focus on the readers who are most likely to buy your book.

As was stated in a previous chapter, **define your target audience:** Analyze your book's genre, themes, and unique selling points to identify the specific group of readers who would be most interested in your content. Consider factors such as age range, demographics, interests, and reading habits to create a clear picture of your ideal readers.

Research your audience: Dive deeper into understanding your readers by conducting market research. Look for trends, preferences, and behavior patterns within your niche. This will help you tailor your messaging and marketing strategies to resonate with your target readers.

Develop targeted marketing strategies: Once you clearly understand your target audience, focus on developing marketing strategies that will effectively reach and engage them. This might include using social media platforms and advertising channels that are popular with your target readers, collaborating with influencers or bloggers in your niche, or taking part in niche-specific events or communities.

Craft interesting messaging: Tailor your book description, website copy, social media posts, and other marketing materials to appeal directly to your readers. Highlight the specific benefits, themes, or elements of your book that will resonate with them and communicate in a tone and style that they will connect with.

Engage and connect with your audience: Actively engage with your target readers through social media, online forums, book clubs, or other relevant platforms. Take part in discussions, respond to comments or questions, and provide valuable content that speaks directly to their interests and needs. Building a connection with your audience can help foster loyalty and word-of-mouth recommendations.

Remember that focusing on your target audience doesn't mean completely ignoring other potential readers. It simply means prioritizing your efforts and resources towards those who are most likely to be interested in and purchase your book. By tailoring your messaging and marketing strategies to appeal directly to this group, you can increase your chances of success and maximize your book's impact.

CHAPTER 18
Using Psychographics to Sell Books

When it comes to selling a book, gathering psychographics can be beneficial for authors. Psychographics go beyond traditional demographics (such as age, gender, and location) and focus on understanding the psychological and behavioral characteristics of a target audience. By gathering psychographic information, authors can gain insights into the values, interests, lifestyles, and motivations of potential readers.

Understanding the psychographics of your target audience can help authors tailor their marketing efforts and messaging to resonate with their readers on a deeper level. For example, if you know your book appeals to readers who value sustainability and eco-friendly living, you can incorporate these themes into your marketing campaigns and tap into the emotions and values of your readers.

Psychographics can also help authors create more relatable and engaging characters and storylines. By understanding the attitudes, beliefs, and preferences of their ideal readers, authors can develop characters and plot elements that resonate with the target audience, increasing the chances of capturing their interest and building a loyal fan base.

However, it's important to note that while psychographics can provide valuable insights, they should not replace a comprehensive understanding of your target market. Authors should still consider other factors, such as demographics, genre preferences, and market trends, when crafting their marketing strategies.

While gathering psychographics can be beneficial for authors to sell their books, it should be done with other market research methods to ensure a comprehensive understanding of the target audience.

Understanding Psychographics
Psychographics go beyond simple demographics to look at the attitudes, interests, opinions, lifestyles, and behaviors of your potential readers. Whereas demographics focus on categories like age, gender, ethnicity, education level, and income, psychographics reveal more about the mindset of your audience.

Some key psychographic factors to consider for your book's target audience include:

Values
What moral principles or belief systems are important to them? What do they care about?

Attitudes
How do they feel about relevant topics related to your book? Are they open-minded or set in their ways? What prejudices or biases might they have?

Motivations
Why might they want to read your book? What problems could it help solve? What goals could it help them accomplish? What desires could it fulfill?

Lifestyles

What hobbies, interests, and activities are they involved in? How do they like to spend their leisure time? What brands and products do they use?

Personalities

Are they introverts or extroverts? Analytical or emotional? Serious or humorous? Optimistic or pessimistic? Understanding personality types can reveal what tone and style of writing will appeal to them.

Really, getting to know your audience's psychographics will help you tailor your book's content, messaging, and marketing to resonate with what matters most to your readers. It takes your understanding deeper than just blunt demographics.

CHAPTER 19
Conducting Market Research

Market research is a critical step in understanding your target audience and determining if there is a demand for your book idea. Before investing significant time and money into writing a book, it's wise to validate that you are solving a real problem or providing value to readers.

There are several methods you can use to conduct market research.

Surveys

Surveys are one of the easiest ways to gather data directly from your potential target audience. You can survey people through email lists, social media, or survey tools like SurveyMonkey. Ask questions to understand their problems, interests, and likelihood of purchasing your book. Get a sense of what they would want to learn or get out of a book on your topic.

Focus Groups

Focus groups involve facilitating an in-depth discussion with a small group of people who represent your target audience. This gives you the opportunity to gain insights by having an open dialogue. Prepare questions to guide the conversation around their needs, problems they face, and how your book idea might provide value. Take detailed notes on feedback.

Interviews

Conduct one-on-one interviews with at least 30 people who match your target reader demographic. Come prepared with questions that reveal their interests, challenges, and thoughts related to your book's concept and contents. Personal interviews allow you to have an in-depth conversation and probe on key insights.

The goal of your market research is to validate you have an audience for your book. Use these findings to refine your book outline and topic coverage. Continuously involve your target readers throughout the writing process to ensure you deliver maximum value.

CHAPTER 20
Analyzing Competitive Books

Before you write your book, it's a good idea to analyze other similar books that are already published. This allows you to better understand the competitive landscape and identify gaps or opportunities that your book could fill.

When analyzing competitive books, look at:

Categories and keywords: What categories is the book listed in? What keywords are used to describe it? This helps you find the right niche for your book.

Reviews: Read through reviews on Amazon, Goodreads, etc. What do readers like or dislike about the book? What do they wish was different or expanded on? Their feedback can reveal weaknesses in existing books you can improve upon.

Author's bio: Research the author, their credentials and platform. How does your background compare? Use their bio as inspiration for crafting your own.

Back matter: Look at the about the author page, acknowledgements, references, and other back matter sections. This can spark ideas for developing your own.

Table of contents: Review the chapter names and structure. What works well that you may want to model? Are there any gaps you could fill?

Book description: Study the book descriptions. See what language and selling points resonate with readers.

Analyzing competitors gives you insights you can use to position your book, distinguish it from others, and make it appealing to your target audience. Familiarize yourself with books like yours so you can both learn from them and improve upon them. This research is time well invested!

CHAPTER 21
Refining As You Write

As you write your book, your understanding of your target audience may evolve. The more you write, the more your ideal reader will come into focus. Don't be afraid to refine your audience's description as your manuscript develops.

For example, you may start out thinking your book is perfect for new parents. But as you delve into the subject, you realize your content is more appropriate for parents with toddlers rather than infants. Or you assumed your book would appeal to both men and women, but use more examples and anecdotes tailored to mothers.

It's perfectly normal for your concept of your reader to become more nuanced as the writing process unfolds. Some characteristics to pay attention to include:

- Age or age range
- Gender
- Marital and family status
- Interests and hobbies
- Reading level
- Personal values and beliefs
- Income level or socioeconomic status
- Geographical location
- Motivations for picking up your book

Stay open-minded and allow your ideal reader to come into a clearer view while you write. Refining as you go will help you shape content that truly resonates with your followers. Just be sure to keep good notes on how your thinking evolves. This will help immensely when it comes time to market your book!

Your market research and audience analysis should directly inform how and where you market your book. Now that you have a clear picture of who your target reader is, you can ensure your marketing efforts are tailored to reach them.

For example, if your book is aimed at business professionals, you'll want to focus on promoting your book through business publications, websites, associations, and events. Run ads on sites frequently visited by your target audience. Attending conferences and networking events to connect with potential readers.

Leverage the demographic and psychographic data you gathered earlier. Create customized messaging and content that will resonate with the age, gender, interests, values, and pain points of your intended audience. Speak directly to their needs and preferences.

You may have multiple segments within your target market. In that case, you can develop slightly different marketing campaigns for each segment. For example, your promotions on Facebook to reach baby boomer women may look different than your Instagram marketing geared towards millennial men interested in the topic.

Monitor which messaging and platforms drive the most interest and engagement from your ideal readers. Double down on those high-performing marketing strategies. Continuously refine based on data and feedback to maximize the relevance and effectiveness of your outreach.

By carefully targeting your marketing to align with your intended audience, you will get your book into the right hands. This ensures the time and money you invest in promotions has real impact. Understanding exactly who you wrote the book for makes all the difference in connecting with readers who will truly appreciate and benefit from it.

Part 3
THE BUSINESS SIDE

Note from the Author: This is probably the section that I get the most questions about. Unless someone has a business of their own, some of the business tasks may leave you feeling overwhelmed. If you are planning on having your books as a business, then you need to consider the items in this section and ask a financial or tax expert for their expertise on the matter.

You also need to remember that when you are selling books directly, you need to pay sales tax to your state. Please check your state requirements for paying taxes on books. The publisher, distribution channels, and other bookstores you work with may take care of the tax for you. Ask the question.

CHAPTER 22
Create A Budget

I t's important to note that the budget will vary depending on factors like the scope of the project, your audience, and your marketing strategy. To create a budget for your book publishing endeavor, consider the following categories:

- Writing and Editing
    - o Writing fees if outsourcing the writing
    - o Editing fees
    - o Proofreading fees
    - o Copyright registration fees
- Design and Formatting
    - o Cover design fees
    - o Interior layout and formatting fees
    - o Illustration or graphic design fees (if needed)
- Printing and distribution
    - o Printing costs, consider both print-on-demand and bulk printing options
    - o Shipping and handling fees
    - o ISBN purchase fee, if needed
    - o E-book conversion fees—if planning to release an e-book

- o Distribution fees for online platforms or retailers
- Marketing and Promotion
  - o Marketing materials (bookmarks, postcards, posters, etc
  - o Website or blog development and maintenance costs
  - o Social media management tools
  - o Advertising and promotional activities (book reviews, giveaways, blog tours, etc.)
  - o Author events or book signing expenses, if applicable
- Miscellaneous
  - o Professional services, such as legal, accounting, etc.
  - o Travel expenses as related to book launches or events
  - o Contingency fund to cover unexpected expenses

Researching specific costs in the publishing industry will help you create a more detailed budget. A publisher will package their services for you, so make sure you understand what is included in their publisher's package.

CHAPTER 23
How to Create a Sales Plan for Your Book

Developing a sales plan for your book involves several steps. Here's a simplified process to help you get started: Identify the specific group of readers who would be interested in your book. Consider their demographics, interests, and reading habits. This will help you tailor your marketing efforts towards them.

Set clear goals: Determine your sales objectives for the book. Define what success looks like to you – whether it's selling a certain number of copies, generating a specific amount of revenue, or reaching a particular bestseller list.

As stated in the last chapter.

Create a budget: Allocate a budget for your marketing and sales activities. Consider expenses such as advertising, promotions, website development, and professional services.

Craft an interesting book description: Write an engaging and enticing book description that captures the attention of potential readers. It should highlight the unique selling points, benefits, and key selling features of your book.

Establish an online presence: Build an author website or create a landing page for your book. You should use these platforms to provide information about yourself, your book, and where it can be purchased. Use social media platforms to engage with readers and promote your book.

Leverage book reviews: Seek credible review platforms and influencers in your book's genre. Positive reviews can significantly impact book sales. Encourage readers to leave reviews on online marketplaces, such as Amazon.

Use email marketing: Build an email list of readers who have shown an interest in your book or genre. Send regular newsletters or updates about your book, upcoming events, and exclusive offers.

Consider book promotions: take part in book promotions and discounted deals to attract new readers. Websites like BookBub and Goodreads offer opportunities to promote your book to their vast user bases.

Engage with your readers: Interact with your readers through social media, author events, book clubs, or virtual author Q&A sessions. Building relationships and engaging with your audience can increase book loyalty and spur word-of-mouth recommendations.

Monitor and adjust: Regularly evaluate the effectiveness of your sales plan by tracking book sales, website traffic, social media engagement, and other relevant metrics. Based on the results, make necessary adjustments to your marketing and sales strategies.

Remember, developing a sales plan is an ongoing process. It requires continuous monitoring, analysis, and adaptation to optimize your book sales.

CHAPTER 24
Create An LLC

D eciding whether to start an LLC for your book business as an author depends on many factors. One consideration includes the potential liability that publishing a book can expose you to, even if you have limited financial success with the book. Lawsuits arising from books can pose a significant financial risk, and having an LLC can provide personal asset protection in such situations.

Another factor to consider is the level of book royalties and business revenue you expect to generate. If your book royalties and/or business income exceed $10,000 per year or you expect to reach that threshold, setting up a corporation or an LLC could be advisable.

Starting an LLC for your publishing company offers the benefit of limited liability for its owners, shielding their personal assets from potential lawsuits and creditors.

It is important to note that starting and managing an LLC involves legal and administrative responsibilities. Consulting with a legal professional is highly recommended to fully understand the implications and benefits specific to your situation.

CHAPTER 25
Select the Retail Price
for Your Book

Pricing your book appropriately is crucial to maximize sales and profitability. Here are a few factors to consider when determining the price:

Understand your target audience: Research the market and analyze the pricing of similar books in your genre. Consider the average price range that your audience will pay for books in that category.

Determine the special value of your book: If it offers exceptional content, has won awards, or has endorsements from renowned individuals, you may justify a higher price.

Production and distribution costs: consider the expenses involved in producing and distributing your book. These may include writing, editing, cover design, printing, eBook formatting, and marketing. Ensure that the price covers these costs and provides a reasonable margin.

Competitive analysis: Consider the pricing strategies of other authors or publishers in your genre. If you choose to price your book significantly higher or lower than the average, be aware of the potential impact on perceived value and competitiveness.

Pricing flexibility: Experiment with different price points to determine the optimal balance between maximizing sales volume and generating revenue. You can consider periodic price promotions or limited-time discounts to attract readers and boost sales.

Early reviews and sales data: Monitor the early response and sales performance of your book. If it is receiving positive feedback and gaining traction, you may adjust the price accordingly to capitalize on its success.

Long-term strategy: Consider the bigger picture and your long-term goals as an author. If you plan to write a series or publish more books in the future, pricing your first book competitively to attract readers can be a viable strategy.

Remember, pricing is not a fixed decision, and you can always adjust it based on market feedback, sales data, and your overall marketing strategy. Regularly reviewing and adapting your pricing strategy will help you optimize sales and revenue for your book.

CHAPTER 26
What Is an ISBN?

ISBN stands for International Standard Book Number. Publishers assign ISBN as a unique identifier to books and related products, which is used worldwide. Every published book typically has its own unique ISBN.

The ISBN is a 13-digit number (previously a 10-digit number) that provides important information about the book, such as its edition, publisher, and format. It helps in identifying and tracking books in libraries, bookstores, and online databases.

As an author or publisher, having an ISBN is important for several reasons:

Identification: An ISBN uniquely identifies your book, making it easier for readers, booksellers, and libraries to find and order your book.

Metadata and Cataloging: ISBNs are used in bibliographic databases, libraries, and online bookstores to organize and categorize books. Having an ISBN ensures your book is included in these databases and can be easily discovered by potential readers.

Retail Distribution: Many book retailers and distributors require ISBNs to sell and distribute books. It is often a requirement for bookstores, online platforms, and distribution networks.

Rights Management: If you plan to sell the rights to your book, having an ISBN can make it easier to track and manage those rights.

Please note that the specifics of acquiring an ISBN can vary by country. To acquire ISBNs, it is often necessary to purchase them from designated agencies or organizations responsible for issuing them.

Overall, an ISBN plays a crucial role in identifying your book, enhancing its discoverability, and facilitating its distribution and cataloging within the publishing industry.

CHAPTER 27
What Is An LCCN?

W hether you need a Library of Congress Catalog Number (LCCN) for your book depends on your specific goals and requirements.

Having an LCCN can be beneficial for authors as it provides an additional level of credibility and recognition for their work. It also allows libraries and bookstores to identify and catalog your book easily in their collections. However, getting an LCCN is not mandatory for all authors, and it is not a requirement for publishing a book or making it available for sale.

If you wish to get an LCCN for your book, you can apply for a Preassigned Control Number (PCN) through the Library of Congress. The PCN program assigns LCCNs to titles before publication and offers cataloging data support.

The decision to get an LCCN depends on factors such as your target audience, marketing strategy, and your desire for your book to be included in library collections. We recommend considering the benefits and potential impact of obtaining an LCCN for your specific publishing goals.

Please note that the specific requirements and procedures for obtaining an LCCN may vary, and it is advisable to refer to the official Library of Congress website or consult with a publishing professional for the most accurate and up-to-date information.

CHAPTER 28
Copyright Your Work

To determine whether you should copyright your work, you need to consider the level of protection you desire for your intellectual property. Copyright provides legal protection by granting exclusive rights to the author or creator of an original work. Here are a few reasons to consider copyrighting your work:

Copyright grants you the right to control how your work is reproduced, distributed, displayed, and performed, providing protection against infringement. If someone infringes upon your copyrighted work, you have legal grounds to take action.

Proof of ownership: Registering your copyright provides evidence of your ownership, which can be useful if someone disputes your authorship in the future.

Licenses and royalties: Copyright allows you to grant licenses to others, giving them permission to use your work in specific ways for royalties or fees.

To copyright your work in the United States, you can apply for registration with the U.S. Copyright Office. The process typically involves the following steps:

- **Determine eligibility:** Ensure that your work meets the requirements for copyright protection, such as being an original creation fixed in a tangible form.

- **Prepare the application** by completing the application forms, which you can do online or through mail. The forms require information about yourself; the work being registered, and the nature of the copyright claim.

- **Submit the application:** pay the required fee and apply to the U.S. Copyright Office. The fee varies depending on the type of work and method of submission.

- **Optional deposit:** While not mandatory, you may choose to submit copies of your work (e.g., a book, manuscript, or recording) as part of the registration process.

- **Wait for processing:** The Copyright Office will review your application, conduct necessary checks, and process your registration.

It is important to note that copyright protection is automatic upon creation of your work, but registering your copyright offers additional benefits and legal protection.

For detailed and up-to-date information on how to copyright your work, including specific application forms and fees, it is advisable to visit the U.S. Copyright Office's website.

CHAPTER 29
What Are Book Royalties?

Book royalties are the earnings that authors receive from the sales of their books. When a book sells, the author earns a percentage of the revenue generated. The percentage, known as the royalty rate, is typically determined by the publishing contract or agreement between the author and the publisher.

Royalty rates can vary depending on factors such as the type of book (e.g., hardcover, paperback, e-book), the sales channel (e.g., retail, wholesale), and the publishing method (e.g., traditional publishing, self-publishing).

In traditional publishing, authors typically receive royalties based on the book's wholesale price or the retail price minus certain deductions (such as returns or distribution fees). Royalty rates for traditional publishing can range from around 5% to 15% of the book's price, although they can be higher for bestselling authors or in certain situations.

Each hybrid publisher has different royalties, these typically range anywhere from about 50%-75% for each book sold. This largely depends on what services are being provided by the publisher and how much the upfront cost is.

In self-publishing, authors often receive higher royalty rates because they have more control over the pricing and distribution of their books. Self-published authors can earn royalties ranging from 35% to 70% of the e-book's sale price, depending on the platform and distribution method.

It's important for authors to carefully review and understand the royalty terms outlined in their publishing agreements. This includes understanding the royalty rate, how it is calculated, any deductions or fees that may be applied, and how the royalties will be paid (e.g., monthly, quarterly). Properly tracking and accounting for book sales helps authors ensure they receive accurate and timely royalty payments.

Authors should also consider that royalties from book sales are typically paid on a schedule defined in the publishing agreement, which may involve a delay, such as monthly or quarterly payments.

Please note that royalty rates and payment terms can vary widely across publishers, publishing methods, and markets, so it's essential to negotiate and review contract terms based on the specific publishing situation.

CHAPTER 30
Ten Things Authors Need to Know About Royalties

These points highlight crucial aspects of book royalties that authors should consider and discuss with their publisher or legal advisor. Ultimately, having a clear understanding of the royalty terms in your publishing agreement is key to managing your earnings and maximizing the financial benefits of your book. Here are ten important things authors need to know about book royalties:

1. **Royalty rates vary:** As stated in the last chapter, royalty rates can differ significantly depending on the type of book, publishing method, and sales channel. It's crucial to understand the specific royalty rates outlined in your publishing agreement.

2. **Negotiating royalties:** In traditional publishing, royalties are typically negotiable. Authors with strong negotiating positions, such as established or bestselling authors, can often secure higher royalty rates.

3. **Advances and royalties:** In traditional publishing, authors may receive an advance against future royalties. Publishers deduct this advance from authors' royalty earnings,

and authors will only receive additional royalties once they have earned out the advance.

4. **Royalties are a percentage:** Royalties are usually a percentage of the book's wholesale price or the retail price, depending on the agreement. It's essential to understand how the royalty percentage is calculated and applied.

5. **Deductions from royalties:** Royalties may be subject to deductions, such as returns, distribution fees, or production costs. Clarify which deductions apply and how they affect your earnings.

6. **Timing of royalty payments:** Royalty payments are typically made on a schedule outlined in the publishing agreement, which can be monthly, quarterly, or annually. Understand the payment schedule and any reporting requirements associated with royalty payments.

7. **Tracking book sales:** Authors should keep track of their book sales to ensure accurate royalty calculations. This can involve monitoring sales reports from publishers or self-publishing platforms and cross-referencing them with royalty statements.

8. **Digital royalties:** E-book royalties can be higher than traditional print royalties in self-publishing or digital-first publishing models. Some self-publishing platforms offer higher royalty rates for e-books, often ranging from 35% to 70% of the sale price.

9. **International Publishing:** Publishing your book internationally may entitle you to foreign rights royalties. These royalties come from sales of translation rights and are negotiated independently from the main publishing deal.

10. **Contractual obligations:** Understand your contractual obligations regarding royalty payments, including any reporting or auditing requirements. It's essential to ensure

that contractual terms align with your expectations and protect your interests.

Please note that these points provide general information, and specific royalty terms can vary widely based on individual agreements and publishing circumstances.

CHAPTER 31
Author Taxes

When it comes to author taxes, there are a few important considerations to keep in mind. If you earn money as an author, whether through book sales or freelance writing, it's essential to understand the tax implications. Here are some key points to consider.

Self-employment income: The Internal Revenue Service (IRS) considers freelance income, and any royalties received from book publishing or self-publishing as self-employment income. This means you'll have to report this income on your tax return and pay self-employment taxes, which comprise both the employer and employee portions of Social Security and Medicare taxes.

Record-keeping: As an author, it's crucial to maintain thorough and accurate records of your income and expenses. Keep track of book sales, royalty statements, and any other sources of income. Save receipts and documentation for any legitimate business expenses you incur, such as research materials or marketing costs. This documentation will help you accurately report your income and maximize deductions.

Deductible expenses: Authors may be eligible for various tax deductions related to their writing activities. Some common deductible expenses include home office expenses, professional association fees, travel expenses for research or conferences, marketing costs, and expenses related to book production. Keep in mind that you must directly relate these expenses to your writing business and document them appropriately.

Estimated quarterly payments: As a self-employed author, you may need to make estimated quarterly tax payments to cover your income tax and self-employment tax liabilities. These payments help ensure you stay current with your tax obligations throughout the year. Failure to make these estimated payments could cause penalties and interest.

Consult a tax professional: because of the complexities of tax laws and individual circumstances, it is advisable to consult a tax professional who specializes in working with authors. They can guide you through the tax planning process, help you maximize deductions, and ensure compliance with tax regulations.

Remember, tax laws can be complex and vary based on individual circumstances and jurisdictions. It's essential to consult with a qualified tax professional or accountant to ensure you're meeting your tax obligations and taking advantage of deductions.

Part 4
EDITING YOUR MANUSCRIPT

Note from the Author: I cannot express how important editors are to our publishing company and the industry. I have edited and proofed this book several times, and I am almost certain that there will still be mistakes that readers will find.

I love using editors so I can just write and get the story out the way I envision it and then someone else can clean it up. Of course, there are so many other reasons to use an editor. It is another set of eyes on your manuscript. They may catch something other than grammar and typos, they may find a hole in your book that you didn't know you had.

So, my heartfelt suggestion is to always invest the money and get your manuscript edited. It is always worth it. But…make sure that you are reading the suggestions and revising what you want. It is ultimately your responsibility for the final approval of the book.

CHAPTER 32
Beta Readers

While not considered an editor, enlisting beta readers can be a great way to get feedback on your writing before publishing or submitting it to editors. This should be done prior to the edit. Here are some steps to help you find and enlist beta readers:

- **Define your ideal reader:** Determine who your ideal readers would be. Are you writing for a specific genre or niche? Knowing your audience can help you find beta readers who are interested in that type of writing.

- **Join writing communities:** Look for online writing communities or forums where you can connect with other writers and aspiring authors. Websites like Goodreads, Wattpad, or writing-specific subreddits can be great places to find potential beta readers.

- **Reach out to fellow writers:** Connect with other writers who might be interested in beta reading for you. You can reach out to fellow writers through writing groups, workshops, or even through social media platforms, like X (formerly known as Twitter) or Facebook groups dedicated to writers.

- **Ask for recommendations:** seek recommendations from fellow writers, friends, or acquaintances who may know people interested in being beta readers. Personal connections can often lead to well-suited beta readers.

- **Create a beta reader questionnaire:** Once you have identified potential beta readers, create a questionnaire to send to them. This will help you gather specific feedback on areas of interest, writing style, and questions you may have regarding your work.

- **Provide explicit instructions:** When sending your manuscript to beta readers, include explicit instructions on what you expect from them in terms of feedback. Ask for honest and constructive criticism and specify any particular areas you would like them to pay attention to.

- **Set a deadline:** Give your beta readers a reasonable timeframe to read your work and provide feedback. Setting a deadline will ensure that you receive feedback in a timely manner.

- **Express gratitude:** Once you receive feedback from your beta readers, thank them for their time and effort. Showing appreciation can encourage a mutually beneficial relationship with potential future beta reading opportunities.

Remember, beta readers are volunteers, so it's important to have realistic expectations and to be grateful for their help.

CHAPTER 33
Questions For Beta Readers

Choose five or six of these questions to give each beta reader. Make sure that you give them a due date as to when you want the information back.

1. **Fiction:** Was the story interesting from the beginning of the book? Why or why not?
    Nonfiction: Was the information interesting from the beginning of the book? Why or why not?
2. **Fiction:** Did you figure out quickly whose story it was? Why or why not?
    Nonfiction: Was the subject easy to understand?
3. **Fiction:** Was there enough intrigue and interest to keep your attention throughout the book? Did you need more?
    Nonfiction: Did the book flow well? Did it stall in parts? Where?
4. **Fiction:** Was there a point in the story where it was slow or where you didn't care to continue on reading? Where?
    Nonfiction: Is there a section in the book that we could remove altogether?
5. **Fiction:** Were there any parts of the books that confused, annoyed, and/or irritated you? If so, which parts? And why?

Nonfiction: Did any of the sections or chapters seem farfetched or not researched well? If so, which parts? And why?

6. **Fiction:** Where there any parts of the story where you noticed inconstancies, weird discrepancies, and or holes in the story? If so, which parts?
    Nonfiction: were any repetitive details in the book?

7. **Fiction:** Did the world in which the story was set bring your enjoyment and did the description adequately capture your imagination?
    Nonfiction: Was the topic exciting for you if you did not know of the topic you were reading about?

8. **Fiction:** Were the characters real? Did they have redeeming qualities? Is there one that could have been better?
    Nonfiction: Could some thoughts and storytelling be better?

9. **Fiction:** Were there too many characters? Were the names too similar or too difficult to remember?
    Nonfiction: Was there too much information or not enough?

10. **Fiction:** Did the dialog hold your interest? Was there too much or not enough?
    Nonfiction: Was the research too lengthy, too boring?

11. **Fiction:** Did you enjoy the ending? Was it believable and did it work with the rest of the story?
    Nonfiction: Did the book provide the next steps?

12. **Fiction:** Did you notice any repeating?
    Nonfiction: Did you notice any repeating?

CHAPTER 34
Get Your Book Edited

G etting your book edited is crucial for ensuring a high-quality, professional, and engaging reading experience. It can enhance the overall quality of your book, increase its credibility, and improve your chances of success as an author. Getting your book edited is important for several reasons.

Improved Quality: An editor can help improve the overall quality of your book by identifying and correcting errors in grammar, punctuation, and spelling. They can also provide suggestions for improving the clarity, flow, and structure of your writing.

Professionalism: A professionally edited book is crucial if you want to be taken seriously as an author. Readers are more likely to trust and engage with a book that editors have carefully edited and polished.

Enhanced Readability: An editor can help you ensure your book is readable and accessible to your audience. They can identify and resolve issues with sentence and paragraph structure, word choice, and overall readability.

Objective Feedback: An editor can provide valuable feedback and insights in your book from an outsider's perspective. They can identify plot holes, inconsistencies, and areas that need further development or clarification.

Increased Credibility: Having your book professionally edited adds credibility to your work. Having your book professionally edited shows your commitment to producing high-quality content and investing in making your book the best it can be.

Competitive Edge: In a saturated book market, having a well-edited book can give you a competitive edge. It can help you stand out from the crowd and increase the chances of attracting readers, agents, or publishers.

Personal Growth: Working with an editor can also be a learning experience for you as a writer. Through the editing process, you can improve your writing skills, learn from your mistakes, and gain valuable insight into the craft of writing.

CHAPTER 35
Types Of Editing

There are several types of book editing, each serving a different purpose in the editing process. Here are five of the common types:

1. **Editorial Assessment:** Sometimes referred to as a manuscript critique, an editorial assessment provides an overall evaluation of the strengths and weaknesses of a manuscript. It offers feedback and suggestions for improvement without changing the text.

2. **Developmental Editing:** Also known as substantive editing or content editing, this type of editing focuses on the overall structure, organization, and content of the book. It involves changing to improve the flow, clarity, and coherence of the story or message.

3. **Line Editing:** Line editing focuses on enhancing the language and style of writing at the sentence and paragraph level. It involves refining the language to make it more engaging, coherent, and interesting.

4. **Copy Editing:** Copy editing involves checking and correcting errors in grammar, spelling, punctuation, and

syntax. It focuses on improving the language and ensuring consistency throughout the book.

5. **Proof Reading:** In the final stage of editing before the book is published, proofreaders carefully check for any errors or typos that may have been missed during previous rounds of editing. Proofreading involves carefully checking for any errors or typos that the previous rounds of editing may have missed.

It is important to note that these types of book editing can overlap, and the specific editing needs may vary depending on the individual project and the expertise of the editor. Professional book editors can provide guidance on which type(s) of editing would be most beneficial for a particular manuscript.

CHAPTER 36
Developmental Editing

D evelopmental editing is a rigorous and collaborative form of editing that focuses on the restructuring of a manuscript, looking at the big picture with a focus on improving narrative flow, structure, pacing, characterization, and overall content and coherence. It is also called substantive or comprehensive editing and occurs before line editing and proofreading.

This type of editing is important for works that show great promise but still need significant rewriting or restructuring. The manuscript may require deep feedback paired with significant revisions. Developmental editing can also be beneficial for authors who need help with concept development or who require detailed guidance on how to craft a polished, cohesive manuscript that meets the standards of their intended audience.

A developmental editor may:

- Assess the work, including evaluating the overarching structure, plot, characters, pacing, tone, and narration.
- Provide feedback on stylistic choices, including voice, point of view, and tense.
- Make suggestions on how to improve character development and character arcs.

- Identify elements of the manuscript that need further development or revision, such as awkward transitions, repetitive sections, or confusing ideas.
- Create an outline or roadmap for revision, which may include structural alterations or suggestions for additional research.

Overall, developmental editing is a critical stage in preparing a manuscript for publication, whether for traditional, hybrid, or self-publishing. It can help to ensure that a work is polished enough to succeed with agents, publishers, or readers.

CHAPTER 37
Line Editing

L ine editing, also known as stylistic editing, is a phase of the editing process that focuses on improving the clarity, flow, and effectiveness of the writing at a sentence level. It involves reviewing and refining the individual lines or sentences in a manuscript to enhance the writer's style and improve the overall readability and impact of the text.

During line editing, a professional editor examines the manuscript sentence by sentence, paying attention to elements such as word choice, syntax, tone, and pacing. The goal is to polish the writing, making it more engaging, coherent, and effective in delivering the intended message or story. Line editing goes beyond grammar and punctuation, emphasizing the stylistic elements that contribute to the overall quality of the prose.

Line editing is not concerned with major structural changes or plot development like developmental editing; instead, it focuses on refining the content without altering its core substance. The aim is to preserve and elevate the writer's style while fine-tuning the writing for clarity, coherence, and impact.

It is important to note that line editing is just one phase of the editing process and typically follows developmental editing, which addresses broader issues such as plot, characterization, and structure.

CHAPTER 38
Copy Editing

Copy editing, also known as manuscript editing, refers to the process of revising written material, known as "copy," to enhance readability and accuracy, while ensuring it is free of grammatical and factual errors. In copy editing, the focus is on refining the text to make it clear and cohesive, while retaining the author's voice and intended meaning.

A copy editor's role involves correcting errors in spelling, grammar, punctuation, and style, as well as addressing issues related to clarity, coherence, and consistency in the written piece. The aim is to improve the overall quality and effectiveness of the written content.

Copy editing differs from proofreading because editors typically perform it after a substantive edit and before the final proofreading stage. While proofreading primarily focuses on surface-level errors and typos, copy editing goes beyond that by ensuring the text flows smoothly, correcting awkward phrasing, improving sentence structure, and offering suggestions for improving overall clarity and organization.

The overall objective of copyediting is to improve the readability and professionalism of the text by polishing it and addressing any inconsistencies or errors prior to publication.

CHAPTER 39
Proof Reading

Proofreading a full-length book involves a careful review and correction of errors in spelling, grammar, punctuation, and consistency. Before publishing the book, proofreading is typically the final step in the editing process.

During proofreading, the proofreader carefully reads through the entire manuscript to identify and correct any spelling mistakes or typos. They also ensure that there are no grammatical errors, properly structuring sentences and using correct punctuation. Proofreaders focus on maintaining consistency throughout the book, checking for errors in formatting, numbering, headings, and other elements.

The goal of proofreading is to ensure that the book is error-free and polished, ready for publication. It is important to note that proofreading does not involve major revisions or changes to the content or structure of the book. Instead, it focuses primarily on fine-tuning the language and fixing any surface-level errors.

We recommend hiring a professional proofreader with experience in book editing to ensure thorough and meticulous proofreading of a full-length book. Professional proofreaders have a keen eye for detail and a deep understanding of grammar and language rules, which allows them to provide a high-quality proof-reading service to authors and publishers.

Part 5

PUBLISHING YOUR MANUSCRIPT

Note from the Author: I have mainly spoken about self-publishing and hybrid publishing. Traditional publishing is another entity all together that has a unique set of items to complete, like finding an agent to represent you, inquiry letters, and researching publishing companies that have open submissions.

If traditional publishing is the route you want to take, don't get discouraged. It takes patience and diligence to publish a book this way, but you can do it.

If you are working with a publishing company to help you self-publish or hybrid publish, the publishing company will handle much of the work for this section. However, I have included common print and publishing terms so you can understand the jargon. Make sure that the company you choose aligns with your goals for your book and for yourself.

CHAPTER 40
Common Print Terms When Publishing a Book

These are just a few examples of common print terms related to publishing a book. There are many more technical and specific terms depending on the type of book and printing process involved.

Advance - Some traditional publishers pay a writer an advance in installments, such as one-half upon signing the contract.

Agent - A liaison between a writer and editor or publisher who advocates for his or her client (writer). Agents usually take a 10-15% commission from the advance and royalties.

ARC - Advance reader copy—an early version of the book sent out to media outlets for reviews and interviews.

Backlist - A publisher's list of its books that were not published during the current season, but that are still in print.

Bimonthly - Every two months.

Bio - A sentence or brief paragraph about the writer can include education and work experience.

Biweekly - Every two weeks.

Bleed - It refers to printing that extends beyond the edge of the page, allowing images or colors to run off the page.

Blurb - The copy on book covers or book dust jackets, promoting the book and the author or featuring testimonials from book reviewers or well-known people in the book's field. Also called flap copy or jacket copy.

Book Spine - When you place the book upright on a shelf, you can see the spine, which is the narrow edge of the book cover.

Bound galleys - Prepublication edition of the book of final galley proofs, also known as "bound proofs."

Byline - Name of the author, appearing with the published piece.

Category Fiction - A term used to include all genres of fiction.

Chapbook - A small print or digital book of poetry or fiction—usually fewer than 40 pages.

Copyediting - Editing a manuscript for grammar, punctuation, printing style, and factual accuracy.

Copyright - A means to protect an author's work.

Cover letter - A brief letter that accompanies the manuscript being sent to an agent or editor.

Cover stock - A thicker and more durable paper used for the cover of the book.

DPI - Dots per Inch, a measurement that determines the resolution or quality of printed images.

Elevator pitch - A concise pitch for a book or screenplay that someone can deliver in the time to travel in an elevator.

End pages - The blank pages glued to the inside of the book cover, used to attach the book block to the cover.

Fair use - Fair use is a provision of the copyright law that allows for the use of brief passages from copyrighted material without infringing on the owner's rights.

Foreign rights - Translation or reprint rights to be sold in other countries and territories.

Frontlist - A publisher's list of books that are new to the current season.

Galleys - They have not yet divided the first typeset version of the manuscript into pages.

Genre - General classification of writing, such as the novel or the poem, or to the categories within those categories within those classifications, such as the horror novel or the sonnet.

Ghostwriter - Writer who writes an article, speech, story, or book based on another person's ideas or knowledge.

Graphic novel - A story in graphic form, long comic strip, or heavily illustrated story; of 40 pages or more.

Gutter - The inner margin or space between facing pages in a book.

Hook - Aspect of the work that sets it apart from others and draws in the reader/viewer.

Imprint - Name applied to a publisher's specific line of books.

ISBN - International Standard Book Number, a unique identification number given to each edition of a book.

Lead time - The time between the acquisition of a manuscript by an editor and its actual publication.

Mass market - Non-specialized books of wide appeal directed toward a large audience.

Memoir - In the memoir, the writer (or fictional narrator) recounts their personal or family history.

MG - Middle grade. The general classification of books written for readers aged nine to 11. Also called middle readers.

Multiple submissions - Sending more than one book, article, or poem to a publisher at the same time.

Narrative nonfiction - A narrative presentation of actual events. Also called creative nonfiction.

Net royalty - A royalty payment based on the amount of money a book publisher receives on the sale of a book after booksellers' discounts, special sales discounts, and returns.

Novella - A short novel or long short story; approximately 7,000 to 30,000 words.

Pen name - Using a name other than your legal name on articles, stories, or books. Also called a pseudonym.

Picture book - Book aimed at preschoolers to 8-year-olds that tells a story using a combination of text and art—or artwork only.

Platform - A writer's quantifiable reach within their target audience, which includes speaking experience, publishing history, social media followers, and more.

POD – Print-on-demand. POD - Print-on-demand is a system or process that prints individual copies or small numbers of a text to order, typically using digital technology.

Proofreading - The act of reviewing a book for errors in grammar, spelling, punctuation, or formatting before it goes to print.

Proposal - Summary of a proposed book submitted to a publisher, particularly used for nonfiction manuscripts. Proposals commonly include a cover letter, a one-page overview of the book, marketing information, competitive books, author information, chapter-by-chapter outline, and sample chapters.

Query - Letter that sells an idea to an editor or agent.

Royalties - A percentage of money that an author receives from a publisher based on sales terms stipulated within a contract.

Self-publishing - In this arrangement, the author pays for manufacturing, production, and marketing of his book and keeps all income derived from the book sales.

Short story - A complete short story of 1,500 words or fewer. Also called flash fiction.

Synopsis - Summary of a story, novel, or play. As part of a book proposal, it is a comprehensive summary condensed on a single-spaced page.

TOC - Table of contents.

Trade book - Book that concerns a special interest for a general audience.

Translation rights - Subsidiary rights for books to be translated and sold in another language.

Trim Size - After trimming down the book from its larger printed form, the book's trim size represents its final dimensions.

Typesetting - The process of arranging text and other design elements on the pages of a book.

YA - Young adult. Manuscripts written for readers aged 12 to 18.

These are just a few examples of common print terms related to publishing a book. There are many more technical and specific terms depending on the type of book and printing process involved.

CHAPTER 41
What is an ARC?

Advanced Reader Copies (ARC), also known as Advance Review Copies or galleys, are early copies of a book that are distributed to readers, reviewers, bookstores, or other industry professionals before the official publication date. Publishers often provide arcs to generate pre-publication buzz and solicit feedback.

The ARC can serve several purposes:

- **Generating reviews:** Authors and publishers provide ARCs to reviewers, bloggers, and influencers in order to generate early reviews and build momentum before the book's release. Positive reviews can help create buzz and attract more readers.

- **Building hype:** By sending out ARCs to influential individuals or building a "street team" of dedicated readers, authors can generate excitement and anticipation for their book.

- **Send out ARCs:** In marketing campaigns, social media promotions, giveaways, or as incentives for preorders or contests, ARCs offer the opportunity for readers to get an early preview. ARCs give readers the opportunity to get an early taste of the book and create a sense of exclusivity.

- **Authors and publishers** can use ARCs to identify any last-minute errors, typos, or formatting issues that may need to be corrected before releasing the final edition of the book. Feedback from readers of ARCs can help improve the final version.

- **Influencing word-of-mouth:** By getting ARCs into the hands of early readers, authors can generate positive word-of-mouth recommendations and create a buzz around their book.

It's important to note that ARCs are typically not the final published version of the book and may contain typographical errors, formatting issues, or other imperfections. Their primary purpose is to generate early feedback and promotion.

CHAPTER 42
Cover Design

The design of the cover of your book is incredibly important for several reasons.

First Impressions: The cover design is often the first thing potential readers see. It plays a significant role in grabbing their attention and enticing them to pick up your book or click on it online. A visually appealing and professionally designed cover can make a strong first impression.

Branding: The cover design helps establish your author's brand and identity. It should communicate the genre, mood, and tone of your book, allowing readers to understand what they can expect from your work. Consistent branding across your book covers can also help build recognition and loyalty among your readers.

Stand Out in a Crowded Market: The publishing industry is highly competitive, and there are countless books vying for readers' attention. A well-designed cover can help your book stand out from the crowd and make it more likely to be noticed and considered.

Book Sales: An interesting cover design can have a direct impact on book sales. It can make potential readers more inclined to purchase your book, whether in a physical bookstore or online.

When working on your book cover design, it is important to consider the audience, genre conventions, and market trends. Researching successful covers within your genre can give you an idea of what works well and help you create a cover that appeals to your intended readers.

If you are not confident in your design skills or don't have experience with graphic design, it may be worth considering working with a professional cover designer or engaging the services of a publishing company. They can create a high-quality cover design that aligns with your book's content and target audience.

Remember, a strong cover design can make a significant difference in capturing readers' attention and generating interest in your book, so it is worth investing time and effort into creating an attractive and impactful cover.

CHAPTER 43
Judging A Book by Its Cover

While it is not accurate to say that *everyone* judges a book by its cover, many people make initial judgments based on the cover of a book. The saying "don't judge a book by its cover" exists for a reason, as it reminds us to look beyond the surface and not solely rely on initial impressions. However, research suggests that visual cues, such as book covers, can influence our expectations and perception of the content inside.

Studies have shown that book covers play an essential role in attracting readers and creating a positive first impression. A visually appealing cover design can grab attention and convey aspects of the book's genre, style, or message. A poorly designed cover may discourage potential readers from giving the book a chance.

While the cover may initially catch the reader's eye, it is important to note that individuals vary in their preferences and can have different reactions to book covers. Ultimately, the decision to judge a book by its cover or delve deeper into its content is a choice.

CHAPTER 44
Hiring A Designer

When hiring a designer for your book cover, there are several factors to consider ensuring you find the right fit. Here are some key considerations.

Portfolio and Experience: Review the designer's portfolio to assess their style, creativity, and skill level. Look for a designer who has experience in designing covers for books in your genre. This can give you confidence that they understand the specific conventions and aesthetics of your target market.

Communication and Collaboration: Effective communication is crucial when working with a designer. Check if the designer is responsive, professional, and open to collaboration. Look for someone who listens to your ideas, provides feedback, and will revise the design based on your input.

Understanding of your Book: Ensure the designer takes the time to understand your book's theme, genre, audience, and key elements that represent your story. The cover should capture the essence of your book and resonate with potential readers.

Versatility and Creativity: A designer should show versatility and creativity in their portfolio. Look for someone who can create unique and eye-catching designs rather than relying on generic templates. This will help your book stand out in a crowded marketplace.

Budget and Timeline: Discuss the project's budget and timeline with the designer upfront. Make sure they can deliver within your desired time frame and provide a clear breakdown of their pricing structure.

References and Reviews: Request references or testimonials from previous clients to gauge the designer's professionalism, reliability, and quality of work. You can also search for reviews or recommendations online to gather additional feedback about their reputation.

By considering these factors, you can find a designer who understands your vision, possesses the skills, and can create an interesting book cover that attracts readers to your work.

CHAPTER 45
Interior Design/Formatting

Interior design plays a significant role in the overall presentation and reading experience of a book. While the cover may initially attract readers, the interior design keeps them engaged as they delve into the content.

Here are a few reasons interior design is important for your book:

Readability: A well-designed interior layout ensures the text is legible and easy to read. Factors like font choice, font size, line spacing, and margins can significantly impact the readability of the text. A comfortable reading experience enhances the overall enjoyment of the book.

Organization: Interior design helps organize the content of the book, making it easier for readers to navigate and find specific sections or information. Elements like headings, subheadings, page numbers, and table of contents contribute to the overall structure and accessibility of the book.

Visual Appeal: Just as a visually appealing cover grabs attention, proper interior design can enhance the aesthetic appeal of your book. Thoughtfully chosen typography, spacing, illustrations, and graphics can improve the visual aspect and make the reading experience more enjoyable.

Consistency: Consistency in design elements throughout the book, such as chapter headings, headers, footers, and formatting, creates a cohesive and professional look. It helps establish a visual identity for your book and maintains a sense of continuity.

Overall, investing in well-thought-out interior design helps create a polished and professional book that attracts readers, enhances the reading experience, and reflects the quality and care put into its content.

CHAPTER 46
Book Types

T here are several types of media formats available for books, depending on your preferences and the platform you intend to use. Here are some common types:

Printed books are the traditional paper format, where publishers physically print the book on paper and bind it together. It allows for tactile reading experience and is widely available.

eBook

E-publishing, also known as electronic publishing, is the process of making digital versions of books, magazines, journals, or any other written content available for distribution and reading through electronic devices such as smartphones, tablets, e-readers, or computers. E-publishing allows for the creation, publication, and distribution of digital content without the need for traditional printing and physical distribution. It has become a popular way for authors, publishers, and content creators to reach a wider audience and offer their work in a more accessible and convenient format.

If you want to do it yourself, to turn your book into an eBook, you can follow these general steps:

- Choose a writing platform or software to write your book. Popular choices include word processors like Microsoft Word or software designed specifically for creating eBooks.

- Use the chosen software to write the content of your book, ensuring that you properly edit and proofread it.

- Organize your content by structuring it into chapters or sections. This will help in creating a clear and logical flow for the readers.

- Design your eBook by adding formatting elements such as headings, subheadings, and paragraphs. You can also consider adding visuals like images and illustrations to enhance the reading experience.

- Convert your book into an eBook format using an appropriate eBook conversion tool or software. These tools will allow you to convert your book into popular eBook formats like EPUB or Mobi.

- Test your eBook on different devices and eBook readers to ensure that it is displaying correctly, and the formatting is intact.

- Choose an eBook publishing platform or service to publish your eBook. Popular options include platforms like Amazon Kindle Direct Publishing, Apple Books, or Smashwords. These platforms will guide you through the process of uploading and publishing your eBook.

- Promote your eBook by creating a marketing strategy that includes online promotion, social media campaigns, and leveraging your existing network. This will help you reach a wider audience and increase the visibility of your eBook.

Remember that the specific steps may vary depending on your chosen writing and conversion tools, as well as the publishing platform you decide to use. It's always helpful to do some research and consult additional resources to ensure a smooth transition from a book to an eBook.

Audiobook

Audiobooks are audio recordings of books, typically with professional narrators, who bring the story to life for listeners. They are audio recordings of books, typically with professional narrators bringing the story to life. Audiobooks allow people to enjoy books while driving, exercising, or engaging in other activities where reading a physical book would be difficult or impossible. They are popular among those who prefer to consume books through listening rather than reading.

Creating an audiobook involves several steps. Here is a general outline of the process.

Select the book: Choose a book that you want to convert into an audiobook. Make sure you have the rights and permission to do so.

Pre-production planning: Determine the budget, timeline, and scope of the project. Decide whether you will narrate the book yourself or hire a professional narrator.

Script preparation: If you're narrating the book yourself, you'll need to create a script or a detailed outline that includes instructions for narration, character voices, and any specific audio cues.

Recording: Set up a quiet recording environment with good acoustics and high-quality recording equipment. If you're recording yourself, make sure to articulate and enunciate your words. If professional narrators are involved, coordinate recording sessions with them.

Editing and mastering: After recording the narration, the audio files need to be edited to remove mistakes, pauses, or any unwanted noises. At this stage, we can add enhancements like background music or sound effects. The files are then mixed and mastered to ensure consistent volume levels and overall sound quality.

Formatting and exporting: Convert the audio files into the format for distribution, such as MP3 or AAC. Make sure the files meet the specifications of the intended distribution platform.

Quality assurance: Listen through the final product to ensure the audio is clear, well-paced, and free of errors. Make any necessary adjustments or corrections.

Metadata and cover art: Prepare metadata, including a title, description, and author information, to accompany the audiobook. Also, design and create cover art that reflects the book's content.

Distribution: Choose a platform or platforms to distribute your audiobook, such as Audible, iTunes, or your own website. Consider both streaming options and download options.

Promotion: Promote your audiobook through various channels like social media, your website, or online platforms dedicated to audiobooks. Seek reviews and feedback to build visibility and credibility.

Remember, the steps may vary depending on your specific needs and resources, and it may be beneficial to consult professionals in the audiobook production industry for guidance.

Paperback Books

A paperback book or perfect bound book is a type of book with a flexible, paper-based cover that wraps around the pages and is glued or sewn to the spine. The pages in a paperback book are typically made of lower-quality paper than a hardcover book, which makes them lighter and more affordable to produce.

Paperback books are often used for fiction novels, academic texts, and other types of books that are intended for a mass-market audience. They are generally less expensive than hardcover books and are easier to carry and transport, making them a popular option for readers who enjoy reading on the go. Because of their affordability and convenience, paperback books are widely available in bookstores, online retailers, and other outlets that sell books.

Keep in mind that the specific steps may vary depending on your preferences and requirements, as well as the printing and distribution options available to you. It's helpful to consult with professionals in the publishing industry or use relevant resources to guide you through the process.

Hardcover Book

A hardcover book, also known as a hardback or hardbound book, is a type of book that has a rigid and durable cover made of thick cardboard or heavy paperboard. The publishers usually wrap a hardcover book in a protective material, such as cloth or leather, and often include a dust jacket that serves as an additional protective layer and provides information about the book.

People know hardcover books for their sturdiness and longevity. Hardcover books typically have pages made of high-quality paper and are bound by sewing or gluing them to the spine. This construction provides added durability and allows the book to withstand repeated use and handling without easily getting damaged or worn out.

Publishers often associate hardcover books with more premium or collector editions, non-fiction books, and literary works, although they also use them for other genres. They have a higher retail price compared to paperback books because of the higher production costs associated with the materials and binding methods used.

People commonly find hardcover books in libraries, bookstores, and personal collections. Hardcover books have an aesthetic appeal and durability that many readers appreciate, often cherishing them as keepsakes or gifts.

The choice of media format depends on factors such as reader preferences, accessibility needs, convenience, and the intended purpose of the book. It is also possible to have your book available in multiple formats to cater to different audiences or platforms.

Seek advice from professionals in the publishing industry or consult relevant resources to guide you through the process effectively.

CHAPTER 47
Print-On-Demand Distribution

Print-on-demand (POD) publishing uses printing technology and a business process where the company prints copies of a book or other documents only after receiving an order. This allows for printing books in single or small quantities, eliminating the need for large stockpiles. With print-on-demand, the company prints books as they receive orders, reducing the cost and risk associated with traditional printing and inventory management. Examples of print-on-demand companies are IngramSpark and Kindle Direct Publishing.

The process of printing on demand includes the creation of digital files for the book, including the text, graphics, and cover. These digital files are then used to print the book when an order is placed. Technology drives this streamlined process, ensuring that publishers print books only when they are needed, reducing waste and enabling authors to easily make updates or reprints when necessary.

Print-on-demand publishing offers several advantages. It allows first-time authors or authors with a list of previously published titles to publish their books easily with no large upfront investments. Print-on-demand eliminates the need for authors or publishers to store and manage inventory, as it prints and ships books directly to customers.

CHAPTER 48
The Importance of Metadata

M etadata plays a crucial role in the sales and discoverability of books. It provides essential information
about a book to potential readers, librarians,
booksellers, and online retailers. Here are a few reasons metadata
is important for book sales:

Discoverability: Metadata helps increase the visibility of a
book by making it easier to find through search engines, online
marketplaces, and library catalogs. Accurate and relevant metadata,
such as title, author, genre, and keywords, improve the chances of
a book being discovered by its target audience.

Categorization and Targeting: Properly categorizing
metadata help ensure that we correctly place a book in relevant
categories, making it easier for readers interested in a specific genre
or topic to find it. This enhances the book's appeal to its target
audience and increases the likelihood of sales.

Online bookstores and retailers depend on metadata to determine the display and recommendations of books on their platforms. Algorithms use metadata to generate personalized recommendations for readers, helping books reach potential buyers who
may be interested in similar titles.

Enhanced Book Descriptions: Metadata provides an opportunity to create interesting book descriptions that entice and
engage potential readers. Well-crafted descriptions, including book

summaries, author bios, endorsements, and reviews, can significantly affect a reader's decision to purchase a book.

Publishing Industry Standard: Many online retailers and book distribution platforms require specific metadata to list and sell books. Adhering to these standards ensures your book meets the requirements for sales channels and avoids potential limitations or rejections.

By optimizing your book's metadata, you increase its chances of being discovered, reaching the right audience, and ultimately driving more sales. It is essential to pay attention to accurate categorization, relevant keywords, and compelling descriptions to maximize the sales potential of your book.

CHAPTER 49
Printing Your Book

If you are an author and planning to get your book printed, here are some things you need to know:

Choose the right printing method: There are several printing methods available, including offset printing, digital printing, and print-on-demand. Each method has its own advantages and limitations, and the best choice depends on the quantity of books you need, budget, timeline, and other factors.

Select the paper type and finish: The type and quality of paper can affect the look and feel of your book. Consider the weight, texture, and color of the paper, as well as the finish, such as matte or glossy.

Pick the book size and format: Select the page size and format that best suits your content, such as paperback, hardcover, or spiral-bound. Consider the layout of the book, including margins, font size, and spacing.

Design the cover: The cover plays a vital role in attracting readers, so it's important to have an eye-catching design that accurately reflects the content of your book. Consider hiring a graphic designer or working with a printing company that offers cover design services.

Get a printing quote: Request quotes from multiple printing companies to compare prices, quality, and printing options. Review the quote details carefully, including the printing lead time, delivery time, and shipping costs.

Proofread and review your book: Before sending your book for printing, make sure it's error free and formatted correctly. Proofread the content multiple times and review the layout, images, and other design elements.

Understand printing terms and concepts: Familiarize yourself with printing terms, such as bleed, resolution, and trim size, to ensure you understand the printing process and can communicate effectively with the printing company.

By understanding these key elements of book printing, you can ensure that your book is printed to your specifications and meets your expectations. It's always a good idea to work with a reputable printing company that can guide you through the process and answer questions you may have.

CHAPTER 50
Publishing Standards

Publishing standards refer to the industry practices or guidelines that publishers adhere to when producing and distributing books. These standards encompass various aspects of the publishing process, including editorial, design, production, and distribution. While these standards can slightly vary between different publishers and genres, here are some key elements often considered:

Manuscript Editing: Editors review and revise manuscripts for grammar, syntax, spelling, and overall clarity to ensure that the content is well written and error-free.

Cover Design: A professionally designed cover that is visually appealing, properly formatted, and aligned with the genre and target audience of the book is essential.

Interior Layout/Formatting: The interior layout of the book, including font selection, line spacing, margins, and chapter headings, should be consistent, legible, and visually appealing.

Copyright: Publishers typically handle the steps to register and protect the copyright of the book on behalf of the author.

The book receives an International Standard Book Number (ISBN) to facilitate tracking, ordering, and sales records.

Printing and Binding Quality: The physical production of the book, including paper quality, print quality, and binding, should meet industry standards to ensure durability and an overall polished look.

Metadata: Publishers provide accurate and comprehensive metadata for the book, including title, author information, genre, and keywords. This metadata helps with book discovery and categorization.

Distribution: Publishers make the book available for distribution through various channels, including online retailers, brick-and-mortar bookstores, libraries, and wholesalers.

Copyright Permissions: If a book includes copyrighted material, such as quotes, artwork, or song lyrics, publishers secure the permissions from the copyright holders for their use.

These are just some of the common publishing standards, and it's important to note that specific standards can vary based on the publisher's policies, genre, and target market. Adhering to these standards helps maintain professionalism and ensures that the final product meets the expectations of readers and industry professionals.

It is advisable for authors to consult specific publisher guidelines or work with professionals, such as editors and designers, who are familiar with industry standards to ensure a high-quality and marketable final product.

CHAPTER 51
Book Distribution

Book distribution refers to the process and logistics of making a book available to readers or consumers. It involves getting the book from the printer or publisher to retailers, libraries, or directly to the readers themselves. The distribution process may vary depending on the publishing method and distribution channels chosen.

For print books, distribution typically involves working with book wholesalers and distributors who handle the storage, warehousing, and shipping of books to retailers. The largest book wholesalers, such as Ingram and Baker & Taylor, play significant roles in distributing books to retailers and libraries.

Online platforms, such as Amazon Kindle Direct Publishing (KDP) or other e-book retailers, enable the distribution of e-books in the digital realm. Authors can reach readers directly through these platforms, as readers can purchase and download digital books online.

Authors can also leverage international distribution by selling translation rights or working with foreign publishers. Self-publishing platforms and global distribution services enable authors to reach a broader international audience.

It's important for authors to understand the distribution process and explore various distribution options to maximize the availability and visibility of their books. Effective book distribution, supplemented by marketing and promotion efforts, can help authors reach a wider readership and increase book sales.

What Authors Need to Know About Book Distribution
As an author, understanding book distribution is crucial for reaching a wider audience and increasing the visibility and availability of your book. Here are some important things you should know about book distribution:

1. **Distribution options:** There are different distribution channels available, including traditional publishing, self-publishing, and hybrid publishing. Each option has its own advantages and considerations, so it is essential to research and choose the most suitable one for your needs.

2. **When working with a publisher:** Publishers have the option of distributing books in various formats, including print books, e-books, and audiobooks. Offering your book in multiple formats allows you to cater to different reader preferences and reach a broader market.

3. **Distribution channels:** Consider the platforms and retailers through which you want to distribute your book. These can include online marketplaces like Amazon, Barnes & Noble, and independent bookstores. Engaging with multiple distribution channels can enhance your reach and visibility.

4. **Wholesalers and distributors:** Working with book wholesalers and distributors helps get your book into physical bookstores and libraries. These intermediaries handle the logistics of distributing your book to retailers and can provide valuable distribution networks.

5. **Marketing and promotion:** While distribution helps make your book available, effective marketing and

promotion strategies are crucial for driving sales and generating interest. Consider investing in marketing activities such as social media campaigns, book signings, author events, and advertising to support your distribution efforts.

6. **Book categories:** Make sure you correctly categorize your book and provide accurate metadata for it. This information helps retailers and readers find your book easily and increases its chances of being discovered.

7. **International distribution and rights:** If you have aspirations for international distribution, explore options for selling translation rights or working with foreign publishers. Alternatively, self-publishing platforms and global distributors can reach international readers directly.

8. **Distribution royalties and contracts:** Understand the financial aspects of distribution, including distribution royalties and contracts. Ensure that you clearly understand how you will receive compensation for sales through different channels and what terms and conditions you are agreeing to.

Overall, thorough research and planning are essential to make informed decisions about book distribution. Consider consulting with professionals or joining author communities and forums to gain additional insights and guidance.

CHAPTER 52
What is a Backlist Book?

Abacklist book refers to a publisher's books that are still in print but have been on the market for at least a year. This term is used to distinguish these older books from newly published titles, which are referred to as frontlist books. The backlist comprises previously published books that are still available for purchase and distribution. These books may continue to generate sales and readership over time, contributing to a publisher's ongoing revenue.

The concept of a backlist is important in the publishing industry, as it represents a valuable asset for publishers and authors. Backlist books often have a proven track record and may have accumulated a dedicated reader base over years or even decades. Publishers and authors can focus their marketing efforts and promotions on backlist books to maintain their visibility and attract new readers.

Publishers may choose to revive interest in backlist books through various means, such as reissuing them with new covers, promoting them through new marketing strategies, or bundling them with other titles. Backlist books can continue to be relevant and profitable long after their initial release, making them a valuable component of a publisher's catalog.

Part 6
MARKETING/SOCIAL MEDIA

Note from the Author: This section could be an entire book in itself. There are a million books on how to market your book—I feel like I have read most of them.

As a publisher, I tried to do marketing and PR for my authors. When I first started, I tried everything, hoping something would stick. This was an expensive and disappointing lesson. It is hard to market a book, but if you have a plan and a good grasp on your target market, you can make it work.

Since learning this lesson, I now offer a six-month social media marketing and PR program to each of my authors. I hired a firm that does both and I am very excited by the outcome.

CHAPTER 53
Plan Your Marketing Efforts

Planning your marketing efforts for your book is essential to ensure that you effectively reach your potential readers and promote your work. Here are some steps to help you plan your book marketing strategy:

Use the information regarding your target audience: Use the information you gathered for who your ideal readers are by considering factors such as age, gender, interests, and reading habits. Understanding your potential reader will help you tailor your marketing efforts to reach them more effectively.

Set clear goals: Define your marketing goals, whether it's increasing book sales, building brand awareness, expanding your author platform, or all of these. Having specific goals will guide your marketing efforts and help you measure their success.

Research your competition: Study other authors and books in your genre or niche to understand what marketing strategies have been successful. This will give you insights and ideas to refine your own marketing approach.

Build your author platform: Establish a strong online presence by creating a professional author website, maintaining active social media accounts, and possibly starting a blog or newsletter.

Engage with your audience: share updates about your writing and create valuable content that resonates with your readers.

Develop a marketing plan: Create a detailed plan outlining the marketing tactics you will use to reach your potential readers. This plan can include strategies like social media marketing, email marketing, book signings, participation in literary events, guest blogging, advertising, and more. Set specific timelines and allocate a budget for each tactic.

Leverage social media: use various social media platforms to promote your book and engage with your target audience. Share interesting content, behind-the-scenes insights, sneak peeks, quotes, and reviews. Interact with your followers and take part in online communities related to your genre or writing interests.

Seek reviews and endorsements: Reach out to book bloggers, influencers, or professional reviewers who specialize in your genre and ask them for reviews or endorsements. Positive reviews and endorsements can significantly boost your book's credibility and visibility.

Build a launch team: Assemble a group of dedicated readers and fans who will support your book launch. These individuals can help spread the word about your book through social media, reviews, and word-of-mouth recommendations.

Plan book events and signings: Organize book signings, virtual author events, or speaking engagements at local bookstores, libraries, or literary festivals. Use online platforms to host virtual book launch parties, webinars, or Q&A sessions to engage with your readers.

Continuous promotion: Remember that book marketing is an ongoing effort. Plan for long-term promotion by consistently sharing updates, engaging with your audience, seeking opportunities for press coverage or collaborations, and exploring additional marketing strategies.

Track and analyze results: Regularly monitor and analyze the results of your marketing efforts. Track book sales, website traffic, engagement metrics, email open rates, and other key performance indicators. This data will help you assess what strategies are working and adjust your marketing plan accordingly.

By thoroughly planning and implementing your book marketing strategy, you can maximize your book's visibility and increase your chances of reaching your desired audience, ultimately leading to greater success for your book.

CHAPTER 54
Your Author Website

Developing an author website is an excellent way to establish your online presence, showcase your work, and connect with readers. Here are some steps to help you develop your author website:

- **Define your website goals:** Determine the purpose of your website. Are you primarily aiming to promote your books, engage with readers, share your writing process, or all of the above? Clarifying your goals will shape the design and content of your website.

- **Choose a domain name:** Select a domain name that reflects your author brand and is easy to remember. You can register a domain through various domain registration websites.

- **Select a website platform:** Choose a website platform that suits your needs and technical abilities. Platforms like WordPress, Wix, Squarespace, or Weebly offer user-friendly interfaces and customizable templates for building your website.

- **Design and layout:** Select a visually appealing and professional website design. Customize the layout, colors, fonts, and images to align with your brand and the tone of your work. Consider using high-quality author photos and book cover images to add visual interest.

- **Create essential pages:** Include essential pages such as a homepage, about the author page, book pages with descriptions and links to purchase, a blog or news section, and contact information. These pages provide relevant information to your readers and make it easier for them to engage with your work.

- **Content creation:** Add engaging and meaningful content to your website. This content could include blog posts, updates about your writing process, book excerpts, author interviews, or any other relevant information for your readers.

- **Make it user-friendly:** Ensure your website is easy to navigate and user-friendly. Organize your content logically and provide clear navigation menus to make it easy for visitors to explore your website. Make sure all links are functional and responsive to various devices.

- **Optimize for search engines:** Implement basic search engine optimization (SEO) techniques to make your website more discoverable. Use relevant keywords in your page titles, headings, and content. Optimize your website's loading speed for a better user experience.

- **Integrate social media:** Connect your website with your social media profiles to cross-promote your content and engage with your audience effectively. Include social media sharing buttons to make it easy for visitors to share your website's content.

- **Regular updates and maintenance:** Keep your website up to date by regularly adding new content, updating book information, and maintaining the functionality of plugins and themes. Regularly check for broken links or outdated information.

Remember that your author website serves as a digital representation of your brand and work, so make sure it reflects your personality and resonates with your potential readers.

Components of Your Author Website

When creating your author website, there are several essential components and information that you should include. Here are some key elements to include on your author website:

- **Homepage:** Create an engaging and visually appealing homepage that introduces visitors to your work. Include a concise and compelling description of your author brand and highlight your latest book or upcoming projects.

- **About the Author:** Provide a page dedicated to introducing yourself and your background as an author. Share your writing journey, your inspiration, and any relevant personal information that helps readers connect with you.

- **Books:** Create individual pages for each of your books, providing detailed descriptions, cover images, and links to purchase them. Include reviews or testimonials to showcase positive feedback from readers or professional reviewers.

- **Blog or News:** Consider having a dedicated blog or news page where you can share updates, writing tips, behind-the-scenes information, author interviews, or any other relevant content. Regularly update this section to encourage return visits.

- **Contact Information:** Make it easy for readers, media, or potential collaborators to contact you. Provide a designated page or include contact information (such as an email address or contact form) on multiple pages of your website.

- **Events and Appearances:** Use a section of your website to share information about upcoming book signings, speaking engagements, workshops, or any other public appearances. Include dates, venues, and additional details to keep readers informed.

- **Media Kit:** Consider creating a media kit that includes your author bio, high-resolution author photos, book cover images, press releases, and any other relevant media materials. Make it easily accessible for journalists, bloggers, or book reviewers who may require this information.

- **Social Media Integration:** Include links or icons that direct visitors to your social media profiles, allowing them to connect and follow you on platforms like X (formerly known as Twitter), Facebook, Instagram, or Goodreads. This helps to grow your online presence and engage with your audience.

- **Testimonials and Reviews:** Highlight positive reviews or testimonials from readers, agents, publishers, or other reputable sources. Positive feedback builds credibility and can attract potential readers.

- **Privacy Policy:** If you collect any personal information from visitors, such as through newsletter sign-ups or contact forms, it's essential to have a privacy policy that outlines how you handle and protect that information.

Remember to regularly update your website with new content, book releases, and events to keep your readers engaged and encourage them to revisit your site. Also, ensure your website design is user-friendly, visually appealing, and reflects your author's brand.

CHAPTER 55
What Is Digital Press Kit?

An author's digital press kit, also known as an electronic press kit (EPK), is a collection of promotional materials and information about the author and their books. It provides media professionals, bloggers, reviewers, and event organizers with comprehensive and easily accessible materials for coverage, interviews, or event planning. Here are some common elements that you may find in an author's digital press kit:

Author Biography: A well-crafted author bio that summarizes the author's background, writing experience, and notable accomplishments.

Book Synopsis: A concise and engaging summary of each book, including the genre, target audience, and main themes.

Author Photos: High-resolution author photos in both color and black-and-white options. These images should be professional, visually appealing, and suitable for various types of media coverage.

Book Covers: High-resolution images of book covers for each published work. These images should be of printable quality and clearly represent the book's design and branding.

Book Excerpts or Sample Chapters: Selections from the author's books that showcase the writing style, premise, and appeal to potential readers.

Author Interviews or Q&A: A list of prepared interview questions and answers that media professionals can use for interviews or to create feature articles about the author.

Reviews and Endorsements: Positive reviews or endorsements from reputable sources, reviewers, or well-known figures in the author's genre or industry.

Media Coverage: A compilation of past media coverage, including links or copies of articles, blog posts, podcasts, or interviews featuring the author.

Contact Information: Clear and updated contact details for the author, including email address, phone number, website, and social media handles. This information should be easily accessible for media professionals to reach out for interviews, review copies, or event invitations.

Event Information: If applicable, details about past and upcoming book signings, speaking engagements, or other public appearances.

Authors should professionally design, organize, and make their digital press kit easily downloadable from their website or share it via a provided link. The goal is to provide a comprehensive resource that makes it effortless for media professionals or event organizers to access the information and materials to feature the author and their books.

Ten Ways to Distribute Your Digital Press Kit

1. **Author Website**: Create a designated page on your author website where visitors can access and download your digital press kit. Make sure the page is easy to find and navigate.

2. **Email**: Send your digital press kit as an attachment or provide a link to download it in your email correspondence

with media professionals, reviewers, bloggers, event organizers, or anyone who requires your press kit.

3. **Author Newsletter**: Include a link to download your digital press kit in your author newsletter. This ensures that your most dedicated readers and fans have access to your press materials.

4. **Social Media Platforms**: Share snippets or highlights from your digital press kit across your social media channels, including Facebook, X (formerly known as Twitter), Instagram, LinkedIn, or any other relevant platforms. Direct interested parties to your website or provide a download link.

5. **Press Release Distribution Sites**: Submit your press kit to online press release distribution sites. These sites often allow you to upload attachments or provide links to your press kit for distribution to media outlets and journalists.

6. **Author Central Platforms**: If you are an author on platforms like Amazon Author Central, Smashwords, or Barnes & Noble Press, include a link to download your press kit in your author profile or book listings.

7. **Virtual Press Kits**: use online platforms specifically designed for creating virtual press kits. These platforms offer customizable templates and allow you to include various media formats, such as images, videos, and sample chapters. Share the link to your virtual press kit across your online presence.

8. **Event Websites**: If you are taking part in book fairs, conventions, or other literary events, check if the event website allows you to upload and share your digital press kit with attendees, event organizers, or potential collaborators.

9. **Digital Publishing Platforms**: If you publish your books through digital publishing platforms such as Kindle Direct Publishing or IngramSpark, consider adding a section in your book's metadata or product description that mentions the availability of the digital press kit on your website or author platform.

10. **Press Kit Distribution Services**: Explore online press kit distribution services that can help distribute your digital press kit directly to journalists, media outlets, and industry professionals. Some services specialize in specific industries, so research and choose the one that fits your genre or target audience.

Remember to keep your digital press kit updated with the latest information and materials and make it easily accessible to anyone who may require it.

CHAPTER 56
Ideas To Market Your Book

Marketing your book can be an exciting and challenging process. Here are some ideas to consider:

Create a website or blog: Establish an online presence where you can showcase your book, share updates, and interact with readers.

Social media promotions: use platforms like Facebook, Instagram, X (formerly known as Twitter), and LinkedIn to engage with your followers. Share enticing content, behind-the-scenes insights, and updates about your book.

Book launch event: Organize a book launch party or virtual event to generate buzz and create an opportunity for readers to connect with you.

Author interviews: Reach out to podcasts, radio shows, and bloggers who might be interested in featuring you and your book as a guest.

Book reviews: Send copies of your book-to-book reviewers or bloggers in your genre to increase exposure and gain valuable feedback.

Guest posting: Contribute articles or guest posts to other websites or blogs in your niche to showcase your expertise and promote your book.

Offer a free sample: Provide a free chapter or brief excerpt of your book on your website or through a newsletter signup to entice readers to purchase the full version.

Book trailers: Create a captivating video trailer that highlights the key elements of your book and share it on your website and social media platforms.

Book signings and local events: Plan book signings at local bookstores, libraries, or literary festivals to meet potential readers and promote your book.

Use online book communities: Engage with platforms like Goodreads, where readers discuss books. Take part in discussions, host giveaways, and build relationships with readers.

Content marketing: Write guest blog posts or articles related to your book's topic and include a link to your book in the author bio or within the article itself.

Paid advertising: Consider investing in targeted online advertising campaigns on platforms like Facebook, Instagram, Amazon, or Google to reach a wider audience.

Book clubs: Reach out to book clubs that focus on your genre and offer to attend their meetings or provide discussion guides to facilitate engagement with your book.

Email marketing: Build an email list of readers and run email campaigns to promote your book, announce events, or share exclusive content.

Collaborate with influencers: Identify influencers or popular figures within your niche and collaborate on promotional efforts, such as hosting joint webinars, interviews, or giveaways.

Remember, the key to effective book promotion is consistency and persistence. Keep promoting your book, even after the initial launch, and try different strategies to see what works best for your genre and target audience.

CHAPTER 57
Book Awards

~

Authors should enter their book into book awards for several reasons. First, winning or even being shortlisted for a book award can provide a significant boost to book sales. The recognition and prestige associated with winning an award can attract attention from readers, media, and industry professionals, increasing awareness and credibility for the book and the author. Winning a book award can serve as a valuable marketing tool, as authors often receive stickers or other visual markers that they can display on the book cover to showcase the book's achievement.

Entering book awards can provide authors with a sense of validation and pride in their writing and career. Winning a respected award can be emotionally rewarding and help to enhance an author's reputation and confidence in their work.

It's important to note that not all book awards have the same impact or credibility. Authors should carefully research and select reputable book awards that align with their genre and target audience. They should review the submission guidelines and requirements to ensure their book is eligible and meets the criteria.

Entering book awards can offer multiple benefits to authors, including increased visibility, credibility, and potential sales.

However, authors should choose wisely when selecting which awards to enter and carefully follow the submission guidelines.

CHAPTER 58
Ten Ways to Support Your Favorite Author

People may ask you what they can do to support your writing career. By supporting you (their favorite author) it is a wonderful way to show appreciation for your work and help you succeed. Here is a list you can give them when then ask.

Ten Ways to Support Your Favorite Author

1. **Purchase their books:** Buying their books, whether in physical or digital format, directly supports the author's work. Consider buying their latest release or even their backlist titles.

2. **Spread the word:** Word-of-mouth recommendations are incredibly powerful. Tell your friends, family, and book clubs about the author and their books. Share your enthusiasm on social media and leave positive reviews on book retail websites.

3. **Attend author events:** Check if the author has any upcoming book signings, readings, or speaking engagements in your area. Attend these events to show support and connect with other fans.

4. **Follow them on social media:** Find the author's official social media accounts and give them a follow. Engage with their posts, leave comments, and share their updates with your own followers.

5. **Request their books at the local library:** If your favorite author's books are not already available at your local library, request for them to be included in the collection. This not only allows more people to discover the author, but also benefits the author through library sales and visibility.

6. **Leave reviews:** Leaving reviews on platforms like Amazon, Goodreads, and other book retail websites can help boost an author's visibility and credibility. Share your honest opinions and discuss what you loved about the book.

7. **Join or start a book club:** Consider starting a book club centered around your favorite author's works. This allows you to discuss the books with others, support the author, and potentially introduce new readers to their work.

8. **Take part in online discussions:** Engage in discussions about the author's books on forums, book review websites, or social media groups. Sharing your thoughts and insights helps generate buzz and encourages others to discover the author's work.

9. **Recommend the author for awards:** If your favorite author's books are eligible for literary awards, consider nominating them or recommending the books to award committees. Recognition from prestigious awards can significantly affect an author's career.

10. **Be an advocate:** Show your ongoing support for the author by advocating for their work. Consider writing blog posts, creating fan art, or organizing virtual events that celebrate the author and their books.

Remember, every action counts, and even the smallest gestures of support can make a difference to an author.

CHAPTER 59
How To Find Marketing Tools That Work for You

When authors are looking for marketing tools that will work for them, it's important to explore different options to find the ones that align with their specific goals and needs. One way to start is by searching the internet specifically for marketing tools for authors. This search can help uncover a variety of resources and platforms that authors can use to promote their work.

Another useful strategy is to consult articles and lists created by industry professionals and experts. For example, SelfPublishing.com provides a comprehensive list of 150 book marketing ideas for authors, offering a wide range of strategies to consider. This list can serve as a valuable starting point for authors to explore various marketing techniques that may resonate with their target audience.

Platforms like Writer's Hive Media and Written Word Media offer lists and articles that specifically focus on free book marketing tools for authors. These resources can guide authors towards cost-effective solutions that can enhance their marketing efforts without breaking the bank.

Overall, authors can find marketing tools that will work for them by conducting internet searches, exploring lists and articles curated by industry professionals, and considering free or cost-effective options provided by reputable sources. It's important for authors to evaluate these tools based on their specific marketing goals and audience, as what works for one author may not work for another.

Here is a list of a few online marketing tools that may work for you.

- Canva
- Book Brush
- Author Lab
- All Authors
- Be Funky
- PicMonkey
- BookBub
- Fuzzy Librarian
- Mail Chimp
- WIX
- GoDaddy
- Word Press

CHAPTER 60
Paid Ads

Paid advertising can be a powerful way to get your book in front of new readers who may not come across it organically. Two major platforms for book promotion ads are Facebook and Amazon Advertising.

Facebook Ads

Facebook offers highly targeted ads based on demographic data and interests. You can tailor your audience by location, age range, gender, interests related to your book topic, and more. Facebook ad campaigns allow you to set a budget and run ads for a specified duration.

When creating Facebook ads, focus on eye-catching visuals and clear, concise copy that conveys the premise and highlights the most interesting aspects of your book. Test different headlines, images, and ad copy to see what resonates most with your readers. Track clicks, engagement, and conversions.

Amazon Ads

Amazon Advertising provides pay-per-click ads targeted to readers searching for books on Amazon. You can bid on relevant keywords so that your ads show up when people search those terms. For example, bidding on keywords related to your book's genre and topic.

Amazon ads are a cost-efficient way to gain more visibility on Amazon and put your book in front of those searching for books just like yours. Make sure your book cover, title and description really stand out, since readers will see them alongside competing ads.

Budgeting for Ads

It's important to set a reasonable advertising budget based on your goals and resources. Unlike organic marketing, paid ads require financial investment. Monitor your daily ad spending and set a monthly budget cap.

As a general guideline, plan for an average cost-per-click between $0.50 and $2 for Facebook and $0.25 and $1 for Amazon. However, costs vary widely based on competitiveness, targeting, and more. Start small, track performance, and allocate more budget to higher performing ads.

Working with Ad Partners

If managing multiple advertising campaigns seems overwhelming, consider working with a digital marketing partner. There are specialists who handle book promotion ads and can optimize and scale your campaigns. They take care of the day-to-day implementation while you focus on your book.

Research partners' expertise, past results for authors, and pricing. Be wary of exploitative deals requiring hefty upfront investment or unnecessary services. A reputable partner will offer transparent, ethical packages tailored to your book's needs.

Paid ads, when done right, can expand your book's reach exponentially. Track them closely to maximize your ad spend and use the data to refine your campaigns. A modest but consistent ad budget over the long-term can keep your book generating interest and sales.

CHAPTER 61
Build A Social Media Platform

A re you an aspiring author trying to promote your book to a wider audience? In today's digital age, having a strong social media presence is crucial for any author's marketing strategy. By building a social media platform specifically tailored to your book, you can connect with readers, build a community, and increase your book's visibility. In this section, we will guide you through the process of creating a social media platform for your book.

Step 1: Know Your Audience

Before diving into the creation of your social media platform, it's essential to identify who your audience is. Understanding who your potential readers are will help you effectively tailor your content and communication strategy to engage with them. Conduct market research to identify demographics, preferences, and reading habits of your audience.

Step 2: Choose the Right Social Media Platforms

With many social media platforms available, it's important to select the ones that align with your book and followers. Facebook, Instagram, X, and Pinterest are popular choices for authors. For example, if your book has visually appealing elements, Instagram and

Pinterest would be ideal platforms to showcase them. Remember that each platform has its own strengths and weaknesses, so choose wisely.

Step 3: Create Your Social Media Handles

Consistency is key when branding your book on social media. Create handles or usernames that are directly related to your book's title or author's name. If your desired handle is unavailable, try adding prefixes or suffixes to make it unique. Having consistent handles across different platforms will make it easier for readers to find and connect with you.

Step 4: Develop a Content Strategy

To engage your audience and keep them interested, plan a content strategy for your social media platforms. Share updates, progress reports, behind-the-scenes insights, excerpts, and quotes from your book. Encourage discussions, ask questions, and respond promptly to comments. Consider creating content related to the themes or topics explored in your book to pique your readers' interest.

Step 5: Engage with Your Audience

Creating a social media platform involves more than just promoting your book. Engage with your audience by responding to comments, thanking readers for their support, and taking part in relevant conversations. Encourage user-generated content by running contests, giveaways, or featuring fanart related to your book.

Step 6: Collaborate with Influencers or Book Bloggers

Collaborating with influencers or book bloggers in your genre can help amplify your book's reach. Reach out to influencers or bloggers who share similar target audiences and ask them to review or feature your book on their platforms. Consider offering free copies or special incentives to secure their collaboration. Their endorsements can significantly boost your book's visibility.

Step 7: Leverage Paid Advertising

Once your social media platform has gained some traction, you may invest in paid advertising to further promote your book. Platforms like Facebook Ads and Instagram Ads provide targeted advertising options to reach specific demographics. Set a budget, define your audience, and experiment with different ad formats to see what resonates with your readers.

Step 8: Monitor and Adapt

Regularly monitor your social media platforms' performance by analyzing metrics such as engagement rates, follower growth, and click-through rates. Use this data to refine your content strategy and adapt to your audience's preferences. Experiment with different content, posting schedules, and engagement techniques to continuously improve your social media presence.

Building a social media platform for your book can be an effective way to establish a strong online presence and connect with readers who are genuinely interested in your work. Remember to maintain consistency, engage authentically with your audience, and adapt your strategy based on their feedback. Embrace the digital world and let your social media platform become a powerful tool in your book marketing journey.

Social Media Prompts to Sell Your Book

When using social media to promote a book, it's important to engage your audience and create meaningful interactions. Here are some effective social media prompts to help sell your book:

Ask trivia questions related to your book: Create engaging posts by asking your followers questions about characters, plot points, or interesting facts from your book. This can pique their interest and encourage them to read or discuss the book.

Share behind-the-scenes content: Give your followers a glimpse into the writing process or the inspiration behind your book. Share photos or videos of your writing space, research materials, or interviews with beta readers or influencers. This helps create a personal connection and generates excitement around your book.

Conduct Q&A sessions: Host live Q&A session on social media platforms, where you invite your followers to ask questions about your book. This not only helps you build a relationship with your audience, but also gives you the opportunity to share more information about your book and generate interest.

Run contests and giveaways: Create contests or giveaways where followers can win a free copy of your book or exclusive merchandise related to it. Encourage them to share their excitement and spread the word about your book on their own social media platforms. This builds buzz and generates user-generated content.

Share reviews and testimonials: Highlight positive reviews or testimonials from readers who have already read your book. Pull out compelling quotes or snippets from these reviews and pair them with visually appealing graphics or images to catch your followers' attention and showcase the quality and value of your book.

Share sneak peeks or excerpts: Tease your followers with sneak peeks of your book by sharing brief excerpts or intriguing quotes. This can create curiosity and anticipation, compelling readers to want to know more and eventually purchase the book.

Create book-related discussions or challenges: Start conversations around themes, topics, or characters from your book.

Ask your followers to share their thoughts or experiences related to these discussions. This creates engagement and encourages followers to explore your book further.

Remember to always include a call-to-action in your social media posts, such as a link to purchase the book or visit your website. Engaging with your audience regularly and providing valuable content will help sell your book and build a loyal reader base.

CHAPTER 62
Facebook

Having a Facebook page as an author can be beneficial for several reasons. Here are some considerations: **Building an author platform:** A Facebook page can serve as a central hub for your online presence and help you build an author platform. It allows you to connect with readers, build a community around your books, and engage with your audience directly.

Reaching a wider audience: Facebook has a large user base, making it a powerful platform to reach a wide audience. By sharing updates, book releases, and engaging content on your page, you can attract new readers and potentially expand your fan base.

Communication and engagement: A Facebook page provides a means to interact and engage with your readers. You can respond to comments, answer questions, and create discussions about your books. This helps build a relationship with your audience and can lead to increased reader loyalty and support.

Sharing updates and promotions: Use your Facebook page to share updates about your writing journey, book releases, book signings, events, and promotions. It serves as a channel to keep your fans and followers informed and engaged with your work.

Advertising opportunities: Facebook offers targeted advertising options that allow you to reach specific audience segments based on demographics, interests, and more. This can be beneficial in promoting your books and reaching potential readers.

However, it's important to note that maintaining a Facebook page requires consistent effort and time. If you decide to create a Facebook page, make sure you have the bandwidth to consistently provide content, engage with your audience, and manage the page effectively.

Ultimately, the decision to have a Facebook page as an author depends on your goals, target audience, and your comfort level with using social media platforms. If you feel it aligns with your marketing and engagement strategy, a Facebook page can be a valuable tool to connect with readers and promote your work.

CHAPTER 63
X (Formerly Known as Twitter)

Having an X (Twitter) account as an author can provide several benefits.

Connecting with readers: X allows authors to connect with their readers in real-time, engage in conversations, and build relationships. It provides a platform to share updates about your writing, interact with fans, and receive feedback on your work.

Building a following: X has a large user base and can help authors expand their reach and gain a following. By sharing interesting content, taking part in writing-related discussions, and promoting their books, authors can attract new readers and fans.

Networking opportunities: X is a platform where authors can connect with other writers, publishers, literary agents, and industry professionals. It offers opportunities to collaborate, learn from others, and stay updated on industry trends.

Promoting books and events: Authors can use X to promote their books, book signings, author events, and other literary activities. By sharing updates, book excerpts, and reviews, authors can generate buzz and attract attention to their work.

Learning and staying informed: X can be a valuable source of information for authors. By following other authors, industry professionals, and literary organizations, authors can stay updated on news, market trends, writing tips, and publishing opportunities.

However, maintaining an active and engaging presence on X requires time and effort. Authors should carefully consider their goals, target audience, and resources before creating an X (formerly known as Twitter) account.

Overall, having an X account can be a valuable tool for authors to connect with readers, expand their audience, and stay connected with the writing community.

CHAPTER 64
LinkedIn

Authors can use a LinkedIn account in many ways to support their writing career. Here are some strategies for authors to make the most of LinkedIn:

Highlight your professional profile: Create an interesting LinkedIn profile that highlights your writing experience, skills, and accomplishments. Include a professional headshot, an engaging summary, and relevant details about your writing journey. This helps establish your credibility as an author and allows you to connect with professionals in the writing and publishing industry.

Connect with professionals in the industry: LinkedIn provides a platform to connect with publishers, literary agents, editors, book marketers, and other industry professionals. Building these connections can open doors to collaboration, networking opportunities, and valuable insights into the publishing world.

Share writing-related content: Use LinkedIn's publishing platform to share blog posts, articles, or insights related to writing, publishing, or your genre. This helps show your expertise, engage with your network, and attracts a professional audience.

Take part in writing and industry-related groups: LinkedIn offers various writing and publishing groups where authors can interact with fellow writers, share knowledge, and engage in discussions. Actively taking part in these groups can help expand your network, gain industry insights, and exchange ideas with other professionals.

Promote your writing and author brand: LinkedIn provides a platform to promote your books, author events, speaking engagements, or workshops. You can share updates, book releases, or guest blog posts related to your writing. Leverage LinkedIn's professional network to amplify your author brand and increase visibility among professionals in the industry.

Seek publishing opportunities: LinkedIn can be an avenue to discover publishing opportunities, such as calls for submissions, writing contests, or anthology opportunities. Join relevant writing or publishing groups, follow literary organizations, and engage with industry professionals to stay updated on potential opportunities.

Remember, LinkedIn is primarily a professional networking platform, so it's important to maintain a professional tone and focus on building meaningful connections within the writing and publishing community.

CHAPTER 65
TikTok

Powerful Ways Indie Authors Can Boost Book Sales Through TikTok. The Introduction to TikTok as a powerful marketing tool for indie authors. Here are some examples:

Unboxing videos: Engage readers by highlighting your book in captivating unboxing videos.

Cover reveals videos: Generate excitement by sharing your book cover on TikTok.

Synopsis summaries: Intrigue potential readers by summarizing the captivating storyline of your book.

Collaborating with book reviewers on TikTok: use the influence of book reviewers to reach a wider audience.

Leveraging bookish trends: Tap into popular book-related trends on TikTok to gain visibility.

Engaging with readers through duets and challenges: Encourage reader participation and engagement through interactive content.

Creating behind-the-scenes videos: Share insights into your writing process, book research, or inspiration to connect with your audience.

Sharing book excerpts and quotes: Tease readers with interesting excerpts and memorable quotes from your book.

Collaborating with other authors: Team up with fellow authors to cross-promote each other's books.

Running contests and giveaways: Generate buzz and attract new readers by organizing TikTok-exclusive giveaways and contests.

Sharing reader testimonials: Leverage social proof by featuring positive reviews and testimonials from readers.

Offering exclusive discounts and promotions: reward TikTok followers with exclusive discounts or limited time offers.

Encouraging user-generated content: Inspire readers to create TikToks related to your book and share their experiences.

Analyzing TikTok insights and adapting strategies: Monitor TikTok analytics to assess the effectiveness of your promotional efforts and refine your approach.

Emphasizing the importance of TikTok as a valuable marketing platform for indie authors and encouraging them to take action.

CHAPTER 66
Instagram

Instagram can be a powerful platform for authors to connect with readers and promote their books. Here are some ways authors can use Instagram to sell their books:

Create an engaging author profile: Set up an Instagram profile that showcases your author brand and books. Use a professional headshot, write a compelling bio, and include a link to your book's website or online store.

Share visually appealing book content: Post high-quality images and videos of your book cover, excerpts, quotes, and behind-the-scenes shots. Use attractive visuals and captions to capture the attention of your audience and pique their interest in your book.

Engage with your audience: Interact with your followers by responding to comments, asking questions, and encouraging conversations. Building relationships with your audience can create a sense of community and loyalty, leading to increased book sales.

Leverage bookstagrammers and influencers: Collaborate with popular bookstagrammers or influencers in your genre. They can help promote your book through features, reviews, or sponsored posts, exposing your work to their engaged followers.

Use relevant hashtags: Research and use popular book-related hashtags to make your posts discoverable to a wider audience. This can increase your visibility and attract readers who are specifically interested in your genre.

Run giveaways and contests: Organize Instagram-exclusive giveaways or contests where participants have to follow, like, or comment on your post to enter. This can help increase your follower count, generate buzz around your book, and potentially increase sales.

Share reader testimonials and reviews: Post positive reviews, testimonials, or user-generated content from readers who loved your book. This social proof can build trust and encourage others to check out your work.

Host live events and Q&A sessions: use Instagram Live or IGTV to host live events, Q&A sessions, or book discussions. This interactive format can deepen the connection with your audience and generate interest in your book.

Collaborate with other authors or book-related accounts: Partner with other authors or book-related Instagram accounts for joint giveaways, shout outs, or cross-promotion. This can help expand your reach and introduce your work to new potential readers.

Use Instagram Shopping: If you have a website or online store, use Instagram Shopping to tag your books in posts or Stories. This feature allows users to make direct purchases through Instagram, simplifying the buying process for your audience.

Remember to consistently post quality content, engage with your audience, and ensure your Instagram presence aligns with your author brand. Instagram can be a valuable tool for authors to connect with readers, build their brand, and ultimately sell more books.

CHAPTER 67
Online Platforms
to Sell Books

There are other platforms available for selling books online. Here are some additional platforms that authors can explore to sell their books:

Amazon: Amazon is one of the largest online marketplaces for books. Authors can self-publish their books through Kindle Direct Publishing (KDP) and sell both digital (e-books) and print-on-demand copies of their books on Amazon.

Barnes & Noble: Barnes & Noble has an online platform called Nook Press that allows authors to self-publish and sell e-books. They also have a print-on-demand service called Barnes & Noble Press for authors who want to sell physical copies of their books.

Apple Books: Authors can publish and sell e-books through Apple Books, which is available on iOS devices. Apple Books offers a wide reach to iPhone and iPad users around the world.

Kobo: Kobo provides a platform for authors to publish and sell e-books. They have a global presence and offer distribution to over 190 countries.

Google Play Books: Authors can self-publish and sell e-books on Google Play Books. It allows authors to reach Android users and users who access Google Play Books through web browsers.

Etsy: While primarily known for handmade and vintage items, Etsy also allows authors to sell physical copies of their books. This platform may be suitable for authors who want to sell limited edition or special edition copies of their books.

Bookshop.org: Bookshop. org is an online platform that supports independent bookstores. Authors can create affiliate links to their books on Bookshop. org and earn a commission from sales, while also supporting independent bookstores.

Smashwords: Smashwords offers a platform for authors to self-publish and distribute e-books. They provide distribution to major e-book retailers such as Apple Books, Barnes & Noble, and Kobo.

Scribd: Scribd is a subscription-based platform that allows authors to publish and monetize their content. Authors can earn royalties based on readership and engagement with their books.

Direct sales through personal websites: Authors can set up their own websites and sell their books directly to readers. This gives authors more control over the sales process and allows for direct communication with readers.

It's important for authors to consider the features, reach, and target audience of each platform before deciding which ones to use. Some platforms may specialize in specific genres or cater to particular reader demographics, so it's beneficial to do thorough research and choose the platforms that align with your goals.

CHAPTER 68
Bookbub

BookBub is a platform that offers book marketing tools and strategies for authors and publishers to help sell more books. It provides promotional opportunities for authors to reach millions of readers who are actively looking for their next book. BookBub offers various marketing tools such as featured deals, discounted promotions, book launch strategies, and advertising options.

Through BookBub, authors can drive preorders, promote new releases, boost sales and visibility, and engage with a community of dedicated readers. The platform allows authors to connect with their target audience and cultivate a dedicated fanbase, which can lead to increased book sales and author visibility.

By utilizing BookBub's marketing tools, authors can benefit from increased discoverability, sales, and rankings on retailer charts and bestseller lists. BookBub also provides authors with free marketing tools to engage with readers and grow their followings.

BookBub has a comprehensive website for authors and publishers, called BookBub Partners, where they can access the marketing tools, find support, and gain insights through the partner blog.

Overall, BookBub is a valuable platform that authors can use to promote their books, engage with readers, and increase their visibility in a crowded marketplace.

CHAPTER 69
Pay Book Reviews

Paying for book reviews can be a controversial practice in the publishing industry. Many reputable book review platforms and websites have strict ethical guidelines that prohibit paid reviews to maintain the integrity of the review process.

However, there are legitimate services that offer editorial book reviews for a fee, providing an objective critique of your book. Professionals who assess the quality, content, and potential marketability of your book conduct these reviews. Here are a few reputable services that authors can consider:

1. **Kirkus Indie Reviews:** Kirkus Indie is a branch of Kirkus Reviews that offers indie authors the chance to have their books reviewed by professional reviewers. There is a fee associated with this service, and the review is impartial and honest.

2. **BlueInk Review:** BlueInk Review provides fee-based professional book reviews for self-published authors and small publishers. Industry professionals who have extensive experience in the publishing and literary world write reviews.

3. **Foreword Clarion Reviews:** Foreword Clarion Reviews specializes in providing high-quality, paid book reviews for

independent authors and publishers. Experienced reviewers write the reviews, and they offer an honest and thoughtful critique of the book.

It is important to note that while these services can provide valuable feedback, paid reviews may not carry the same weight or influence as unbiased reviews from readers or reputable publications. Building a strong readership, receiving organic reviews, and engaging in genuine marketing efforts are often more effective in gaining credibility and promoting your book.

Remember, authenticity and integrity are crucial in the publishing world, and readers appreciate genuine feedback and recommendations.

CHAPTER 70
Create A Seasonal Promotion

Creating seasonal promotions is an effective way for authors to engage with readers, boost sales, and create a sense of excitement around their books. Here are some steps to help you create seasonal promotions:

Identify relevant seasons and holidays: Research and identify seasons, holidays, or special occasions that align with the themes or settings of your book. For example, if your book is set during Christmas, consider creating a promotion around the holiday season.

Set clear goals: Determine what you want to achieve with your seasonal promotion. Are you aiming to increase book sales, gain new readers, or generate buzz around your work? Setting clear goals will help you shape your promotion strategies.

Create special offers or discounts: Develop enticing offers or discounts specifically tailored to the seasonal promotion. This could include discounts on the book's price, bundles with other related products, free shipping, or exclusive bonus content. Make sure the offer is compelling and valuable to potential readers.

Plan promotional activities: Consider different marketing activities to promote your seasonal offer. This might include social media posts, email newsletters, blog posts, guest appearances on podcasts, interviews, or collaborations with other authors or influencers in your genre. Leverage these channels to create awareness and drive traffic to your promotional offer.

Use seasonal aesthetics: Incorporate seasonal visuals into your promotional materials. Create eye-catching graphics or book covers that reflect the colors, symbols, or imagery associated with the season or holiday. This helps create an emotional connection and attracts potential readers.

Engage with your audience: Interact with your readers through social media, email, or other communication channels. Encourage them to share their favorite seasonal book recommendations or host discussions and contests related to the season. Engaging with your audience builds a sense of community and keeps readers interested and involved in your promotion.

Collaborate with other authors: Consider partnering with other authors in your genre to create joint promotions or cross-promotions. This can expand your reach, introduce your work to new audiences, and create a sense of excitement within your shared fan base.

Leverage book signing events: If you have scheduled book signing events during the seasonal period, use these occasions to promote your seasonal offer. Offer special incentives or exclusive signed editions to attendees and encourage them to spread the word.

Track and analyze your results: Monitor the performance of your seasonal promotion by tracking sales, website traffic, engagement metrics, or customer feedback. This will help you understand what worked well and what areas could be improved for future promotions.

Adapt and learn: Based on your analysis, take note of successful strategies and learn from any challenges faced during the promotion. Use this knowledge to refine your promotional plans for future seasonal campaigns.

Remember, seasonal promotions should align with the themes of your book and resonate with your target audience. By engaging readers and creating a sense of excitement, you can effectively leverage seasonal opportunities to increase book sales and build a loyal fan base.

Another idea is to use National Days to sell your books. Researching and leveraging national days can be a great way to promote book sales. By aligning your book with specific national days or observances, you can tap into existing conversations and reach a wider audience. Here are some steps to help you research national days to sell your books:

Start with general research: Conduct an internet search for "national days" or "national observances" to find lists of special days, weeks, or months celebrated nationally. Websites like National Day Calendar and National Today provide comprehensive lists of national observances throughout the year.

Identify relevant days: Look through the lists and identify national dates or themes that align with the topics of your book. For example, if you have written a children's book about animals, World Wildlife Day on March 3rd might apply to your promotion.

Plan your promotions: Once you have identified relevant national days, brainstorm creative ways to tie your book into those days. Consider offering discounts, running giveaways, or creating special content related to the national day. For example, if your book is a romance novel, you could offer a special Valentine's Day promotion.

Leverage social media: Use social media platforms to promote your book with the national days. Create engaging posts highlighting the connection between your book and the national day, and use relevant hashtags to reach a broader audience. Engage with your followers by encouraging them to share their experiences related to the national day and your book.

Collaborate with influencers and bloggers: Reach out to influencers or bloggers who have a niche audience interested in the national day or topic of your book. Offer them a free copy of your book or propose a collaboration to create content that promotes both the national day and your book. This can help to expand your reach and generate buzz.

Plan: Keep a calendar of upcoming national days throughout the year and plan your promotions well in advance. This will allow you to create engaging content and ensure you have enough time to prepare and execute your promotional activities effectively.

Remember, while national days can provide opportunities for book promotion, it is essential to align your book's content genuinely with the national day to maintain authenticity and relevance.

CHAPTER 71
Facebook Live to Promote Your Books

Authors can use Facebook Live as a powerful tool to promote their books and engage with their audience. Here are some tips on how authors can use Facebook Live for book promotion:

Q&A Sessions: Conduct live question-and-answer sessions where readers can ask questions about your book, characters, or your writing process. This creates a personal and interactive experience and helps build a connection with your audience.

Live Readings: Share live readings from your book during a Facebook Live session. This allows your audience to experience your writing style and hear excerpts directly from the author.

Book Launch Events: Host a special Facebook Live event to launch your book. Include behind-the-scenes insights, sneak peeks, and exciting announcements to generate buzz and excitement among your followers.

Author Interviews: Invite other authors or experts in your genre for live interviews. This not only provides valuable content to your audience but also helps cross-promote each other's work.

Exclusive Content: Offer exclusive content or giveaways during Facebook Live sessions. For example, you can give away free copies of your book, offer signed copies, or provide behind-the-scenes insights that are not available anywhere else.

Collaborate with Influencers: Partner with influencers or book bloggers who have a large following and host a joint Facebook Live event. This helps you reach a wider audience and tap into their established fan base.

Cover Reveals: Unveil your book cover during a Facebook Live session. This creates excitement and anticipation among your audience and generates interest in your upcoming release.

Book Discussions: Host a live book club discussion on Facebook Live, where readers can join and share their thoughts about your book. This creates a sense of community and encourages engagement with your work.

Remember to promote your Facebook Live sessions to your audience in advance and engage with them during the broadcast by responding to comments and questions. This helps create a more interactive experience and strengthens the connection with your readers.

CHAPTER 72
Contact Book Clubs

There are several ways authors can contact book clubs to introduce their books and potentially arrange for author visits or discussions. Here are some methods you can try:

Local Chamber of Commerce and Parks & Recreation: Contact your local chamber of commerce or parks and recreation department and inquire if they are aware of any organizations or local book clubs in your area.

Google Search: Conduct a simple Google search using your location name followed by "book club." This search can often provide a list of local book clubs you can reach out to.

Bookstores: Check with your local bookstore to see if they host book clubs or if they have recommendations for book club picks. They might connect you with book clubs that meet at their store or help facilitate discussions.

Book Club Directories: use book club directories such as BookClubCookbook, which connects authors and publishers with book discussion group members.

Online Communities and Platforms: Join online book club communities and platforms, such as Goodreads or Facebook groups, focused on books and reading. Engage with members, share information about your book, and express your interest in connecting with book clubs.

Author Websites and Contact Forms: Visit author websites and look for their contact page. Many authors provide an email address or contact form where you can reach out to inquire about potential book club engagements.

Remember to be respectful and provide a clear and concise introduction of yourself and your book when reaching out to book clubs. Mention any relevant information, such as availability for author visits or discussions.

It's important to note that while these methods can help you contact book clubs, there is no guarantee of a response or invitation. It's always a good idea to approach book clubs with a genuine interest in their reading community and a willingness to contribute to their discussions.

CHAPTER 73
Sell Themed Product

Authors can sell themed products associated with their book to engage with their readers and generate additional revenue. Here are some ways authors can accomplish this:

Merchandise or Swag: Create merchandise like t-shirts, hoodies, mugs, or tote bags featuring book cover art, quotes, or characters. These items allow readers to showcase their support for the book and become walking advertisements.

Book-related Accessories: Develop accessories that align with the theme or setting of the book. For example, if the book has a fantasy setting, consider selling bookmarks, jewelry, or keychains that draw inspiration from the magical elements in the story.

Art Prints and Posters: Commission or create art prints or posters that highlight key scenes or beautiful book cover illustrations. Fans of the book can sign and sell these as collectible items.

Book-inspired recipes or Cooking Products: If your book contains food references or recipes, consider creating a themed cookbook or selling cooking products such as aprons, recipe cards, or spice blends. These can offer a unique and immersive experience for readers.

Exclusive Editions or Box Sets: Create special editions of the book with bonus content, exclusive artwork, or additional stories. Bundle several books together into a box set with unique packaging and offer it as a limited-edition item for fans.

Digital Extras: Develop digital extras such as bonus chapters, short stories, or companion guides that provide additional context or backstory to the book. You can sell these as eBooks or offer them as incentives for pre-orders or newsletter sign-ups.

Collaborations with Artists or Crafters: Partner with artists, illustrators, or crafters to create handmade items that align with the book's theme. This can include custom artwork, handcrafted bookmarks, or custom-designed bookplates.

Book-inspired Workshops or Events: Organize workshops, classes, or events related to the book's theme. This could range from writing or art workshops to guided tours of locations featured in the book. Offer tickets or access to these events as a themed product.

When selling themed products, authors can set up an online store on their website or use established e-commerce platforms like Etsy or Shopify to showcase and sell their merchandise. Use social media, author newsletters, or book launch events to promote and drive sales of the products.

Keep in mind that the production and distribution of physical products may require additional logistics and financial investment. It's important to research and plan accordingly to ensure a successful and profitable venture.

CHAPTER 74
Contact Bookstores

The best way for authors to contact bookstores may vary depending on individual preferences and the specific bookstore you are trying to reach. Here is a recommended approach that can increase your chances of getting a response:

Research the Bookstore: Start by researching the bookstore you wish to contact. Visit their website and social media profiles to gather information about their events, author policies, and relevant contact details.

Email or Contact Form: Email is typically the preferred method of communication for many bookstores. Look for the bookstore's email address or contact form on their website. Write a professional and concise email introducing yourself and your book. Customize each email for the specific bookstore, mentioning any connections or reasons you believe your book would be a good fit for their store and readers. Inquire about the possibility of arranging an event, signing, or consignment. Attach a press kit or relevant information about your book, if applicable.

Be sure to carefully follow any specific guidelines or instructions for author submissions or event proposals provided by the bookstore. Ignoring guidelines may cause your email being overlooked or discarded.

Phone Call: Another option is to follow up your email with a phone call. Call during the bookstore's business hours and ask to speak with the events manager or the person responsible for author events. Be prepared with a brief script about your book and why it would be a good fit for their store. Make a polite inquiry about the possibility of arranging an event or signing.

In-Person Visit: If the bookstore is local and open to in-person visits, consider introducing yourself and your book in person. Ask to speak with the events manager or the person in charge of author relations. Have a copy of your book or a professional press kit to leave behind.

Networking: Attend book industry events, conferences, or trade shows where you can connect with bookstore owners, managers, and event coordinators in person. Building relationships and networking within the industry can lead to future opportunities and recommendations.

Independent Bookstore Associations: Check if there are any local independent bookstore associations in your area. These associations may have a directory or resources that can help you connect with multiple independent bookstores at once.

Remember to be respectful, professional, and patient when contacting bookstores. Understand that bookstores receive many inquiries from authors, so it may take time for them to respond or consider your request. Tailor your approach to each bookstore, showcasing why your book would benefit their readers and community.

Consider targeting a mix of independent bookstores and chain bookstores, as they may have different submission processes and event opportunities.

Ultimately, persistence and a well-crafted pitch can help you stand out and increase the likelihood of establishing positive partnerships with bookstores.

CHAPTER 75
How To Promote Your Book on Preorder

To promote a book on preorder, here are some actions an author can take.

Build anticipation: Create buzz around your book by building anticipation leading up to the release date. Share snippets, teasers, or behind-the-scenes information on your social media platforms or website.

Engage with your audience: Interact with your readers by responding to comments, messages, or emails. Engaging with your audience can create a connection and build excitement for your book.

Offer exclusive content: Provide incentives to readers who preorder your book, such as exclusive bonus chapters, signed bookmarks, or access to a private Q&A session. This will give them an added reason to preorder early.

Use social media: Leverage platforms like Facebook, Twitter, Instagram, and YouTube to promote your book. Share updates, post visuals, and build a community around your book by engaging with your followers.

Collaborate with influencers: Partner with influencers, bloggers, or booktubers who have an audience that aligns with your target readers. They can help create awareness and generate interest in your book.

Encourage reviews: Reach out to your existing readers, friends, and family members to leave honest reviews on platforms like Amazon or Goodreads. Positive reviews can attract more readers and increase the visibility of your book.

Leverage your network: Ask for support from your network of friends, family, and colleagues. Request them to share preorder links and help spread the word about your book.

Guest blogging or podcasting: Seek opportunities to be a guest on relevant blogs or podcasts to talk about your book. This can help you reach new audiences and showcase your expertise as an author.

Offer preorder discounts or incentives: Provide a special discount or incentive for readers who preorder your book. This can motivate them to secure a copy early and create a sense of urgency.

Host a virtual launch event: Plan a virtual launch party or event to celebrate the release of your book. This can include a live reading, Q&A session, or even a giveaway. Promote the event on social media to attract attendees.

Remember, consistency and engagement are key in promoting your book on preorder. Continuously share updates, interact with your audience, and provide valuable content to keep the momentum going until the release date.

CHAPTER 76
Pre-Launch Marketing Strategies

In the months leading up to your book's launch date, there are several key strategies you should focus on to generate buzz and momentum.

Build Excitement with ARCs: One of the most important pre-launch activities is getting advance reader copies (ARCs) into the hands of book reviewers, influencers, and engaged readers. ARCs allow you to generate buzz and collect reviews well before your launch date.

Identify relevant book reviewers and influencers who align with your genre and topic and pitch them to receive an ARC. Be sure to follow submission guidelines and only send to those likely to provide an honest, quality review. Services like NetGalley can distribute digital ARCs at scale for a cost.

As reviews come in, share them on your author website and social media. Positive early reviews will validate your book and generate further interest.

Run a Preorder Campaign: Allow readers to preorder your book in the months leading up to release. This helps boost initial sales numbers and propel momentum on launch day.

Set up your preorder pages on major retailer sites. Promote the preorder pages through your website, email list, and social channels. Consider offering special preorder bonuses or discounts to incentivize early buys.

Preorders show real demand for your book and allow retailers to gauge interest. Strong preorder numbers can help your book garner further in-store promotions and visibility.

Start Publicity Outreach Early: Identify relevant media outlets, podcasts, book bloggers, and influencers for potential publicity opportunities around launch time. Pitch them early with your book details and ARCs.

Look for angles that connect your book to current events or trends. Time interviews and guest posts around your launch date for maximum exposure.

Pre-launch publicity outreach takes time, so start reaching out 4-6 months before release. Follow up regularly and politely. Record outreach details to stay organized and strategic.

With smart pre-launch marketing, you can hit the ground running once your book is finally available. Build that critical buzz and validation through early reviews, visibility boosts from preorders, and launch publicity.

Part 7
THE BOOK LAUNCH & BEYOND

Notes from the Author: This is one of the most important sections for this message alone. Don't stop marketing your book. Even though the publishing industry could mark it as backlist after six months or a year, that doesn't mean you have to stop selling it. Many books have a long and illustrious run.

CHAPTER 77
Planning Your Launch Sequence

A successful book launch requires careful planning and co-ordination of key launch activities leading up to and on your release date. Here are some tips for planning an impactful launch:

Coordinate release day actions:

- Upload your final manuscript to publishing platforms at least one week before launch. This ensures no delay in your book going live on sites like Amazon.
- If you are working with a publisher, check on the completion date before you schedule your book launch.
- Let your network know the exact release date and ask them to buy and review your book on launch day. Line up post shares and publicity.
- Schedule social media posts and ads to go live on launch day. Space out your posts throughout the day.
- Plan a launch event or online party. Rally fans to attend and spread the word.
- Leverage Amazon advertising.
- Set up your Amazon Author Central profile and claim your book page.

- Enroll in Amazon Ads and create a sponsored product campaign leading up to and during launch.
- Bid higher on launch days to gain more visibility and momentum. Monitor and optimize daily.
- Plan media and publicity pushes.
- Identify media targets like book reviewers, bloggers, podcasts and pitch them with copies of your book, press releases, and personalized pitches.
- Line up guest posts, interviews and other publicity opportunities to coincide with launch.
- Promote media mentions through social media and collect assets like podcast episodes to share.

Careful planning of your launch sequence will help generate that crucial momentum and visibility when your book first goes live. Leverage advertising, media outreach, events and your network to make a splash on release day. Maintain energy in the days and weeks following launch to capitalize on interest.

CHAPTER 78
How To Plan a Book Launch Party

Planning a book launch party involves several key steps. Here is a guide to help you plan a successful book launch event:

- **Determine the date and venue:** Choose a date and time that allows for ample preparation and promotion leading up to the event. Select a venue that can accommodate the expected number of attendees and suits the style and theme of your book.

- **Define the purpose and goals:** Clarify the purpose of your book launch party. Is it to celebrate the release, attract media attention, or increase book sales? Set specific goals to guide your planning process.

- **Create a budget:** Plan and allocate a budget for your book launch party. Consider expenses such as venue rental, decorations, refreshments, marketing materials, and any pre-event promotions.

- **Develop a guest list:** Identify and invite individuals who are likely to be interested in your book, including family, friends, colleagues, local influencers, bloggers, book reviewers, and members of your audience. Consider collaborating with other authors for a joint launch party to expand your reach.

- **Send out invitations:** Send out formal invitations that reflect the theme and tone of your book. Use digital invitations, physical mailed invitations, or a combination of both. Include key details like date, time, venue, RSVP information, and any special instructions.

- **Plan the program:** Create a timeline and plan out the program for the book launch event. Consider elements such as a speech or reading by the author, a book signing session, a Q&A session, or any other interactive activities that align with your book's theme or message. Keep in mind the time needed for guests to socialize and mingle.

- **Arrange for multimedia and promotional materials:** Prepare any audiovisual materials, such as a book trailer or presentation, to showcase your book during the event. Consider having promotional materials such as bookmarks, business cards, or flyers available for attendees to take home.

- **Decorate the venue:** Decorate the venue in a way that reflects the tone and theme of your book. Use props, book covers, banners, or other decorations that enhance the ambiance of your event. Create a visually appealing space for guests to enjoy.

- **Catering and refreshments:** Plan and coordinate refreshments that align with the theme of your book launch party. Consider providing small bites, themed cocktails/mocktails, or a dessert table. Make sure to consider dietary restrictions or preferences.

- **Publicize the event:** Promote your book launch party through various channels, including your website, social media platforms, email newsletters, local event listings, and press releases. Engage with local media outlets or bloggers to maximize coverage and attendance.

- **Follow up:** After the event, send thank-you notes or emails to attendees, express gratitude to any sponsors or supporters, and share highlights or photos from the event on your social media platforms or website.

- **Track book sales and feedback:** Monitor book sales and gather feedback from attendees. This can provide valuable insights into future marketing and promotional efforts.

Remember, each book launch party is unique, so tailor your planning process based on your book's genre, audience, and personal preferences. Focus on creating a memorable, engaging event that leaves a positive impression on your attendees.

CHAPTER 79
Book Launch Team

An author's book launch team is a group of dedicated individuals who come together to support the author in promoting and launching their book. These individuals can be friends, family members, colleagues, or even fans who are enthusiastic about the author's work and want to contribute to its success.

The primary role of a book launch team is to help spread the word about the book and generate buzz leading up to and during the book's release. Here are some common tasks that a book launch team may undertake:

- **Social Media Promotion**: Book launch team members can help promote the book on their own social media platforms, sharing announcements, excerpts, cover reveals, and pre-order links. They can also engage with the author's posts by liking, commenting, and sharing them to increase their reach.

- **Book Reviews**: Book launch team members may commit to reading and posting honest reviews of the book on retail sites like Amazon, Goodreads, or personal blogs. Positive reviews are essential for building social proof and encouraging potential readers to purchase the book.

- **Beta Reading and Feedback**: Some book launch team members may offer to be beta readers, reading an early version of the book and providing valuable feedback to the author. This feedback can help the author refine their manuscript before publication.

- **Sharing Promotional Materials**: Book launch team members can help distribute promotional materials, such as bookmarks, flyers, or postcards, in their local communities, bookstores, or libraries. This physical presence can help generate interest in the book and drive potential readers to purchase it.

- **Organizing Events**: Book launch team members can help plan, organizing, and promoting book launch events, such as parties, signings, or readings. They can help secure venues, invite guests, handle logistics, and promote the event to ensure a successful turnout.

- **Online Engagement**: Book launch team members can actively engage in online book communities, such as book clubs, forums, or Facebook groups, by recommending the book, taking part in discussions, or organizing virtual events like author Q&A sessions or book club discussions.

- **Word-of-Mouth Promotion**: Members of the book launch team can help create buzz by talking about the book with their friends, family, and colleagues, both online and offline. Personal recommendations can be powerful in generating interest in the book and expanding its reach.

- **Supporting the Author**: Book launch team members can provide emotional support and encouragement to the author throughout the book launch process. They can cheer the author on, celebrate milestones, and help manage the workload associated with book promotion.

It's important for an author to build a book launch team with individuals who are genuinely enthusiastic about their work and willing to commit time and effort to help promote the book. Timely communication, clear expectations, and expressing gratitude for the team's contributions are essential for maintaining a positive and productive working relationship.

By leveraging the collective efforts of a book launch team, an author can maximize the visibility and success of their book launch, ultimately reaching a wider audience and attracting more readers.

CHAPTER 80
Day of Book Release

The day of a book release is a very important day for an author. Here are some things an author can do on the day of their book release:

Share the news on social media: Use social media platforms like Twitter, Facebook, and Instagram to announce the release of the book. Share the book cover, a link to where people can purchase it, and any relevant hashtags related to the book or genre on social media platforms like Twitter, Facebook, and Instagram.

Email subscribers: If an author has a mailing list, they can send out an email to their subscribers to let them know about the book's release. This is a great way to reach a targeted audience who has already shown an interest in the author's work.

Schedule interviews: Book releases often generate media attention, so authors should schedule interviews with radio shows, podcasts, or book bloggers to talk about the book and promote it to a wider audience.

Host a launch party: If an author has a local community and has established relationships with local bookstores or libraries, they can consider hosting a launch party or book signing event. This can be a great way to celebrate the book with friends, family, and fans.

Monitor online activity: On the day of the book release, an author should monitor online activity, including social media mentions, reviews, and sales rankings. They can use this information to track the book's performance and make any necessary adjustments to their promotional strategy.

Overall, the day of a book release should be a day to celebrate the accomplishment and hard work that went into creating the book. By using various strategies to let the world know about the book's release, an author can make a big splash and share their story with the world.

CHAPTER 81
Post-Launch Momentum

The initial launch of your book is just the beginning. The momentum and excitement you generate around the launch are key to driving ongoing interest and sales. Here are some ways to keep that momentum going:

Following Up on Media Opportunities:

Don't let media opportunities pass you by

- Make a list of relevant media outlets and journalists who may be interested in your book. Reach out with a pitch and follow up. Look for opportunities like writing guest articles or being interviewed.
- Send follow-up emails to any media contacts you pitched before launch with an update on your launch success. Provide them with any interesting launch metrics or reviews. Make it easy for them to cover your book.
- Look for tie-ins to current events or news that may make your book timely for media outlets to cover again.

Getting Reviews

- Ask satisfied readers to leave reviews on sites like Amazon and Goodreads. Provide them with links or instructions on how to leave reviews.

- Reach out to book reviewers, influencers and bloggers in your genre and offer them review copies. Getting additional quality reviews helps build credibility.
- Share great reviews on social media and via your mailing list. Quotes from reviews make great promotional material.

Speaking Engagements

- Use the authority and exposure from your book launch to connect with event planners. Offer to give talks or workshops related to your book's subject matter.
- Look for speaking opportunities at conventions, community centers, bookstores, libraries, business associations, networking events, etc.
- Convert your book's core topics and lessons into speeches, presentations or actionable takeaways for audiences.
- Speaking allows you to connect directly with readers and buyers and expands your influence. It also gives you more content to share and keep audiences engaged.

The key is to keep finding creative ways to get your book in front of new readers. Leverage every opportunity to generate ongoing buzz. Maintaining momentum takes continued effort but helps extend the book's lifespan.

CHAPTER 82
Ongoing Promotions and Discoverability

O nce your book is published, the work doesn't stop. You want to keep promoting your book and making it discoverable to new readers long after the initial launch. Here are some effective ongoing promotion strategies:

Giveaways and Promotions

Run free or discounted giveaways on platforms like BookFunnel, StoryOrigin, or BookFun.net. This expands your reach and helps you gain new readers.

Offer your book as part of bundle deals or boxed sets around certain themes, topics, or genres. Cross-promote with other authors in your niche.

Pitch your book to include in promotional newsletters, websites, or apps like BookBub, BookGorilla, or Hoopla. The increased visibility can drive sales.

Organize a blog tour to connect with readers on other sites. Offer guest posts, interviews, excerpts, reviews, or giveaways to bolster interest.

Pitch your book-to-book reviewers on book review sites, blogs, YouTube channels, podcasts, and more. Getting more reviews helps credibility and SEO.

Backlist Marketing

Promote your previously published books to readers of your new releases. Cross-link between books on your website and social media.

Offer the first book in a series at a discount or for free to incentive readers to buy the rest of the series at full price.

Bundle your backlist titles together in boxed sets or compilation editions, which can tap into new readers.

Run occasional countdown deals, promotions, or limited-time discounts on your backlist books to boost visibility.

Advertise your backlist in author newsletters, on your website, and across your social media channels regularly. Out-of-sight is out-of-mind.

Optimizing Metadata

Refine your book metadata, categories, and keywords periodically to help with discoverability. Check how your book looks on vendor sites.

Update or expand your book description and bio when you have new information that's relevant.

Add awards, reviews, blurbs, or new information about your author brand into your book's marketing copy.

Research keywords that are driving sales in your niche and integrate highly searched terms organically into metadata and marketing.

Take advantage of opportunities to improve visibility, like Amazon's A+ Content or Author Central profile. Optimize everywhere you can.

By actively keeping your book visible and discoverable with ongoing promotions, you can continue reaching new readers and sustaining sales long after launch. Don't let your book disappear into the ether—keep marketing!

CHAPTER 83
Expanding Your Reach

After you publish and launch your book, you will be able to take advantage of additional opportunities to expand its reach to new audiences globally. Some key ways to increase exposure and tap into new markets include:

Translations

Having your book translated into other languages can introduce your content to a whole new set of potential readers. Identify which foreign languages have the biggest market opportunity based on your book's topic and audience. Work with a professional translation service to ensure high-quality translations that properly convey the meaning and spirit of your original text. You can publish and distribute translated versions of your book through the same or different publishers in international markets.

Audiobooks

Creating an audiobook version opens up your book to a listener base who prefer the audio format. Audiobooks expand accessibility for those unable to read print versions because of vision impairment or learning disabilities. They are also convenient for busy people to play during commutes or while multi-tasking. Producing an audiobook requires a significant investment, including hiring a professional narrator and dealing with production logistics. However, this additional format can pay dividends by attracting new readers.

Foreign Rights
Licensing rights to publish your book in other countries is an effective method for entering new geographical markets. Identify countries where your book's subject matter is likely to resonate with readers. Research publishers who specialize in your genre and have an established reach in target foreign markets. Negotiate contracts to sell the rights for translated editions, working through the legalities and financial details. Be prepared to promote the book across borders through visits, interviews, and other marketing outreach customized for each country.

Pursuing these tactics for amplification requires significant effort, but the reward is introducing your book to more people worldwide. With strategic planning and execution, translations, audiobooks, and foreign rights can extend the impact of your work beyond the original publication.

CHAPTER 84
Tracking And Evaluating Results

O nce your book is published, it's important to track various metrics and data points to understand how your marketing efforts are performing. This allows you to identify what's working well so you can double down on those strategies. It also helps reveal where there's room for improvement.

Sales Data

Your book sales metrics will be one of the most important indicators of success. Be sure to monitor your sales regularly across all platforms and sales channels where your book is available. Look at daily, weekly, and monthly sales numbers. Analyze how sales respond after new marketing pushes and track performance after launches and promotions. Set sales goals and aim to grow your readership.

Online Analytics

Make use of online analytics to gain insights about how people are discovering and engaging with your book content. If you have a website or author platform, use Google Analytics to view traffic sources, what content people are visiting, audience demographics, and more. Monitor your social media engagement and follower growth. Track website conversions and email list sign-ups. See which affiliate links and promotions are driving the most referrals.

Surveys and Feedback

Getting direct feedback from readers is invaluable. Consider sending surveys to ask what readers enjoyed most, what they'd like to see more of, how they found your book, etc. Look at reviews and ratings on retailer sites. Engage with readers on social media and in your email list. See what people are saying in discussions about your book. Be open to both positive and constructive feedback so you can continue improving. Listen to what your audience wants next.

Analyzing this data over time provides powerful insights that allow you to refine your approach. Track trends to spot what's working and identify new opportunities to connect your book with more readers.

CHAPTER 85
Author Blogging and Blog Tours

Writing a blog about their book allows authors to connect with readers, promote their work, and share insights about the writing process. Here are some steps authors can follow to write a compelling blog about their book:

- **Identify the purpose:** Determine the goal of the blog post. Do you want to share behind-the-scenes details, discuss the inspiration behind your book, or provide writing tips? Clarifying the purpose will help you structure the content.

- **Target your audience:** Consider who your intended readers are. Are they fans of your genre or aspiring writers? Understanding your audience will help tailor your content to their interests and needs.

- **Choose a captivating headline:** Craft a catchy headline that grabs the reader's attention and hints at what they can expect from the blog post. Make it engaging and relevant to the topic of your book.

- **Provide an introduction:** Begin your blog post with a captivating introduction that hooks readers and establishes why they should continue reading. You can mention key aspects, such as the book's genre, main themes, or unique elements.

- **Share your writing journey:** Readers enjoy getting a glimpse into an author's writing process. Discuss the inspiration behind your book, the challenges you faced, or interesting research you conducted. This personal touch can create a deeper connection with readers.

- **Discuss key themes or characters:** Share insights into the main themes or characters of your book. Explain why these elements are important and how they contribute to the overall story. Avoid giving away too many spoilers; instead, focus on creating curiosity.

- **Include excerpts or teasers:** Consider including short excerpts or teasers from your book to give readers a taste of your writing style or an intriguing moment from the story. This can entice readers to want to learn more.

- **Engage with readers:** Encourage readers to leave comments or ask questions at the end of your blog post. Respond to comments promptly, fostering a sense of community and building relationships with your readers.

- **Promote your book:** Don't forget to include a call-to-action at the end of the blog post, guiding readers to where they can purchase your book or find more information about it. You can also mention any upcoming book signings, events, or promotions.

- **Edit and proofread:** Before publishing your blog post, ensure it is well-edited, free of errors, and easy to read. Consider having someone else review it for feedback and suggestions.

- **Share your blog:** Once you publish your blog post, promote it on your social media platforms, author website, and through your mailing list. Engaging with your audience through these channels can amplify your message.

Remember to make your blog posts informative, engaging, and authentic. By sharing your passion for your book and connecting with readers, you can generate interest and build a loyal fan base.

How to Plan Your Blog Tours

Authors can schedule blog tours to promote their books and reach a wider audience. Here are some steps to help with scheduling a blog tour:

- **Research book bloggers:** Look for book bloggers whose readership and content align with your audience. Consider factors such as blog traffic, engagement, niche focus, and previous reviews of books in your genre. Compile a list of potential blogs to approach.
- **Get in touch with bloggers:** Reach out to the bloggers on your list to inquire about their interest in hosting your blog tour. Write a personalized and concise email introducing yourself, your book, and the purpose of the tour. Provide relevant information such as book synopsis, release date, format options (e.g., eBooks, paperback), and any additional materials you can provide (e.g., author interview, guest post, book excerpt).
- **Offer incentives:** To increase the likelihood of bloggers taking part in the tour, consider offering incentives. These can include free copies of your book, exclusive content or

giveaways for their readers, or even compensation if it aligns with your budget.

- **Coordinate the tour schedule:** Once bloggers ask about hosting your tour, work with them to schedule specific dates for each blog post. Keep in mind the length and desired duration of the tour, typically ranging from one to four weeks.

- **Provide blog tour materials:** Send bloggers the materials for their posts, such as relevant images, author bio, book cover images, and any specific content requested (e.g., guest post topics, interview questions). Ensure they have everything they need to create engaging and informative content about your book.

- **Prepare unique content:** To make each blog post unique and enticing for readers, offer different content for each blog stop. This can include author interviews, guest posts, book reviews, excerpts, character interviews, or even giveaways. Providing diverse content will keep readers engaged throughout the tour.

- **Follow up and promote:** As the blog tour dates approach, follow up with the bloggers to confirm their posts are on schedule. Promote each blog post on your social media channels and author website, tagging and thanking the bloggers for their participation.

- **Engage with readers:** Engage with readers in the comment sections of each blog post. Respond to comments, answer questions, and show appreciation for their support. This interaction will help build a connection with potential readers and create a positive impression of your book and your author's brand.

Remember, effective communication, organization, and collaboration with the taking part bloggers are essential for a successful blog tour. By harnessing the reach and influence of book bloggers, authors can effectively promote their books and generate interest among their target audience.

CHAPTER 86
How Authors Can
Get on Podcasts

To get on podcasts as an author, there are several strategies you can employ:

- **Pitch yourself directly:** Instead of relying on a publicist, consider pitching yourself directly to podcast hosts. Most podcast hosts receive many generic pitches, so crafting a personalized and compelling pitch can increase your chances of getting booked.

- **Research podcasts:** Identify podcasts that align with your book's genre, themes, or followers. Listen to episodes, get familiar with the podcast's content and style, and consider how your book would fit within their topics. Look for contact information or submission guidelines on the podcast's website.

- **Offer value to the audience:** Highlight how your book or expertise can provide value to the podcast's audience. Explain what unique insights or perspectives you can contribute to the discussion. Focus on how your book can entertain, educate, or inspire the listeners.

- **Build connections:** Networking with podcast hosts or taking part in podcasting communities can help you get on podcasts. Attend industry events, join social media groups, or engage with podcasters through platforms like Twitter or LinkedIn. Building relationships can lead to invitations or recommendations for podcast appearances.

- **Prepare a media kit:** Create a professional media kit that includes your author bio, book synopsis, high-resolution book cover images, and any media or press reviews you have received. Make this readily available on your website or include it in your pitch to podcast hosts.

- **Be a podcast listener:** Familiarize yourself with the podcasts you want to appear on by listening to episodes and becoming a fan of the show. Show genuine interest in the podcast and show your familiarity during the pitch. Engaging with the podcast host and audience can help establish a connection.

- **Leverage your network:** Look for connections in your network who have been guests on podcasts or know podcast hosts. They may be able to provide introductions or recommendations, increasing your chances of getting booked.

Remember, each podcast is different, so tailor your approach to fit the specific podcast and its audience. Put effort into crafting an interesting pitch that showcases your expertise and the value you can provide to the listeners.

CHAPTER 87
Join Forces with Other Authors

Authors can work together to cross promote their books in the following ways.

Online collaborations: Guest blog posts, interviews, or joint giveaways are effective ways for authors to reach each other's audiences. Consider partnering with authors who write in a similar genre or have a complementary audience.

Social media shout outs: Authors can give each other shout outs on social media platforms by tagging their fellow authors and recommending their books to their followers. This can help increase visibility and reach a wider audience.

Bundle promotions: Create themed book bundles with other authors and promote them as a package deal. This can be done for limited-time promotions or as a joint offering to promote each other's work.

Review exchanges: Authors can exchange honest reviews of each other's books on platforms like Goodreads or Amazon. Positive reviews from fellow authors can lend credibility and attract more readers.

Giveaway collaborations: Organize joint giveaways where authors contribute copies of their books or other related goodies.

This can increase participation and expose both authors to each other's fan bases.

Book signings or events: Coordinate book signings or virtual events with other authors. Pooling resources and promoting the event collectively can attract a larger audience and generate more interest.

Collaborate on anthologies: Create an anthology with multiple authors contributing short stories or novellas. This can expose each author to the other contributors' fan bases and provide an opportunity to cross promote each other's books.

Newsletter swaps: Partner with other authors to include a mention or feature about each other's books in your newsletters. This allows you to reach a targeted audience who has already shown an interest in your work.

Joint advertising: Consider pooling resources to run shared advertisements or promotions in relevant publications, newsletters, or websites. This allows for wider exposure and cost-sharing.

Supportive communities: Join author communities or groups where authors actively take part in cross promotion. These groups often focus on supporting and promoting each other's work.

Remember, when collaborating with other authors, it's important to approach it as a mutually beneficial partnership. Communication, reciprocity, and a genuine interest in promoting each other's work are the keys to successful cross promotion.

CHAPTER 88
How To Schedule Book Signings

Remember to be professional, polite, and persistent when reaching out to bookstores. Some may receive many requests, so it may take time to secure a spot. To schedule book signings, you can follow these steps:

- **Contact bookstores:** Begin by reaching out to bookstores in the target area where the signing would take place. Look for local independent bookstores, as well as larger chain bookstores. You can usually find contact information on the bookstore's website or by calling their main line.

- **Prepare a pitch:** When contacting bookstores, be prepared to provide a brief pitch about your book, highlighting its unique features and why it would be a good fit for their store. Mention any previous accolades, positive reviews, or relevant experience you may have as an author.

- **Offer promotional opportunities:** Bookstores are more likely to host a signing if they see an opportunity for mutually beneficial promotion. Offer to share the event on your social media channels, blog, or email newsletter. You could also propose collaborating on advertising efforts or reaching out to local media for coverage.

- **Determine logistics:** Discuss dates, times, and other logistical details with the store. Be flexible and accommodating, as bookstores might already have a full calendar of events. Consider scheduling signings around weekends or during high-traffic periods to maximize attendance.

- **Consider multiple locations:** If you will travel, reach out to bookstores in different cities or regions to expand your book signing opportunities. This can help you reach a wider audience and potentially increase book sales.

- **Coordinate with a publicist or agent:** If you have a publicist or literary agent, they can help you navigate the process and establish connections with bookstores. They may also handle scheduling and logistics on your behalf.

After confirming the dates and locations, make sure to promote the book signing to your fans and followers. Use social media, email newsletters, your author website, and any other platforms you have to spread the word. Encourage attendees to bring friends and family to further increase attendance.

CHAPTER 89
How To Get Libraries to Buy Your Books

To get libraries to buy your book, you can try the following strategies.

Research libraries: Start by identifying libraries that would be a good fit for your book. Look for libraries that have a collection in your genre or cater to your readers. Check their catalog or website to see if they already have similar books in their collection.

Contact librarians: Reach out to librarians in the libraries you have identified. Send them a polite and concise email introducing yourself and your book. Mention why you think your book would interest their library patrons and how it fills a gap in their collection. Offer to provide them with additional information or a review copy of your book.

Attend library events: Attend local library events such as author readings, book club meetings, or writing workshops. This will help you connect with librarians and establish a relationship with them. Networking and building personal connections can increase the chances of your book being considered for purchase.

Offer author visits or workshops: Libraries often invite authors to give talks or conduct workshops. Pitch yourself as a speaker to libraries, emphasizing your expertise or unique perspective. This can be a great opportunity to showcase your book and generate interest among the library staff and patrons.

Use library purchasing processes: Many libraries have a process for patrons to request books to be added to their collection. Encourage your readers or fans to request your book at their local libraries. Sometimes, libraries prioritize purchasing books that receive multiple requests from their patrons.

Leverage reviews and awards: Positive book reviews and awards can enhance the appeal of your book to libraries. If your book has received favorable reviews from reputable sources or has won any awards, mention this when contacting libraries. Positive reviews and recognition can increase the perceived value of your book.

Remember, getting libraries to buy your book may take time and persistence. Keep reaching out to libraries and building relationships with librarians and be patient with the process.

CHAPTER 90
Printed Materials

Remember to allocate a budget for printed materials and consider working with professional designers and printing services to ensure high-quality and visually appealing materials. While digital marketing is crucial, printed materials add a tangible element to your book promotion efforts, reinforcing your book's presence and increasing its discoverability in both online and offline spaces.

Printed materials are beneficial for authors for several reasons.

Tangible and Memorable: Printed materials, such as bookmarks, postcards, or flyers, provide a physical representation of your book that readers can hold and keep. Unlike digital content, printed materials allow for a tactile experience, leaving a lasting impression on potential readers.

Offline Marketing: While digital marketing is essential, printed materials allow authors to reach readers in offline spaces, such as bookstores, libraries, or community events. By distributing printed materials in these settings, authors can tap into a broader audience and attract potential readers who may not be as active in online spaces.

Promotional Tools: Printed materials serve as promotional tools that can be easily distributed and shared with others. You can distribute bookmarks and postcards at book signings, attach them to giveaway prizes, or leave them in local businesses to create opportunities for more people to discover and be intrigued by your book.

Visual Appeal: Well-designed printed materials can catch the eye and pique curiosity. By investing in professional graphic design, authors can create visually appealing materials that align with the tone, theme, and branding of their book. This visual appeal can help make your book more memorable and stand out among other promotional materials.

Enhanced Discoverability: Printed materials can include essential information about your book, such as the title, cover art, blurb, author bio, and purchase details. By providing all the details in a visually appealing format, potential readers can easily and conveniently discover your book.

Support for Events: Printed materials are especially valuable for author events, such as book launch parties, signings, or readings. They serve as decorations, handouts, or giveaways that organizers can use to engage with attendees and maintain a connection with them beyond the event.

Personal Touch: Handing someone printed material, such as a signed bookmark or a postcard with a personalized message, creates a personal and intimate connection between the author and the reader. This personal touch can leave a lasting impression and make the reader feel valued and interested in exploring your book.

Marketing Collateral for Partnerships: When collaborating with local bookstores, libraries, or organizations, having printed materials can be valuable for partnership opportunities. Sharing the printed materials with these partners can help create awareness and generate sales when they display or distribute them.

CHAPTER 91
Ideas to Get Book Reviews

Remember that it's essential to approach potential reviewers respectfully, provide them with a quality book, and appreciate their time and effort. Not all review requests will cause reviews, but by utilizing a combination of these strategies, you can increase the chances of receiving valuable reviews for your book. Here are ten different ways that an author can get reviews for their book:

1. **Reach out to Friends, Family, and Colleagues**: Start by reaching out to people you know and ask if they would read and review your book. Friends, family members, and colleagues are often supportive and can provide honest feedback.

2. **Use Book Review Bloggers**: Research and reach out to book review bloggers who specialize in your genre. Many book bloggers accept review requests and may be interested in reviewing your book on their blog or website.

3. **Join Online Author/Reader Communities**: Engage with online communities where authors and readers congregate. Platforms such as Goodreads, Reddit, and book-related forums provide opportunities to connect with

readers interested in leaving reviews. Just be sure to follow community guidelines and avoid spamming.

4. **Offer Advanced Reader Copies (ARCs)**: Provide free copies of your book to a select group of people in exchange for an honest review. These can be individuals who have expressed interest, loyal readers, or members of your launch team. ARCs help generate early buzz and can cause reviews upon publication.

5. **Contact Book Reviewers**: Research book reviewers who cover books in your genre and actively review independently published works. Reach out to them, following their submission guidelines, and offer a digital copy or paperback for review consideration.

6. **Consider paid review services, but exercise caution and thoroughly research them to ensure their legitimacy, transparency, and adherence to ethical guidelines.**

7. **Offer Giveaways**: Create buzz and encourage reviews by running book giveaways on platforms like Goodreads, social media, or your website. Encourage participants to leave a review after reading the book.

8. **Collaborate with Book Clubs**: Reach out to local book clubs or online book club communities and offer to provide discussion questions or take part in virtual author Q&A sessions. Engaging with book clubs increases the likelihood of receiving reviews from club members.

9. **Request Reviews from Influencers**: Identify influencers or industry professionals in your genre who have a considerable following. Reach out to them with a personalized message, offering a free copy of your book for review, and explain why you think they would enjoy it.

10. **Run a Limited-Time Discount or Free Promotion**: Temporarily discount or offer your book for free to boost visibility and attract readers who may leave reviews after reading. Promote the promotion through social media, newsletters, and relevant platforms.

CHAPTER 92
Should You Do Amazon Ads?

A uthors should run Amazon ads as it can be beneficial for promoting their books. Amazon Advertising is a unique platform that allows authors to advertise their titles where most readers are actively searching and purchasing books. By utilizing Amazon ads, authors can place their books in front of a targeted audience that is already interested in making a purchase. The sponsored product ads appear in search results when users search for relevant keywords, increasing visibility and potentially driving more sales.

One advantage of Amazon ads is that authors can get thousands of impressions for free. Since Amazon charges on a pay-per-click basis, authors have the opportunity to have their ads displayed to a wide audience, incurring no cost if people choose not to click on the ad. This exposure alone can create brand awareness and potentially drive sales.

However, it's important for authors, especially new authors, to approach Amazon ads with a strategic mindset. It is essential to understand and track the results of the ad campaigns to ensure they are getting a return on their investment. By setting a budget and monitoring the performance of the campaigns, authors can optimize their ads to reach the right audience and maximize the impact of their advertising efforts.

Running Amazon ads is not a guarantee of success, and authors should carefully evaluate their marketing goals, budget, and target audience before deciding to invest in Amazon ads. It may be helpful to further research best practices and take advantage of resources provided by Amazon to maximize the effectiveness of the ad campaigns.

CHAPTER 93
What Are the Best Types of Ads for Your Book?

For determining the best types of ads for your book, it depends on various factors, such as your audience, budget, and marketing goals. Here are a few types of ads that authors commonly used to promote their books:

- **Digital Ads**: These include online advertisements on platforms like Amazon, Facebook, Google Ads, and other relevant websites. Digital ads allow you to reach a wide audience and provide tracking capabilities, making it easier to measure the effectiveness of your campaigns.

- **You can run print ads through newspapers, magazines, catalogs, and other physical media.** While digital ads have become more prevalent, print ads can still be effective for reaching certain demographics and creating brand awareness.

- **Book Review Bloggers**: Partnering with book review bloggers who specialize in your genre can help generate buzz and increase the visibility of your book. These bloggers have a dedicated following of readers who trust their recommendations, making it an effective way to reach potential readers.

- **Influencer Marketing**: Collaborating with influencers or industry professionals who have a significant online presence can help promote your book to their followers and expand your reach. This could involve sponsored social media posts, author interviews, or guest blog posts.

- **Book Trailer or Video Ads**: Creating a visually appealing book trailer or video ad can capture the attention of potential readers and provide a glimpse into your book's content. You can share these ads on social media platforms, book-related websites, or even during video streaming services.

- **Newsletter Promotions**: using newsletters targeting readers in your genre can be an effective way to promote your book and drive sales. Many authors offer exclusive discounts or bonuses to subscribers, encouraging them to purchase and review the book.

It's important to note that the effectiveness of each advertising method may vary depending on your specific book, target audience, and marketing strategy. Experimenting with different ads and tracking the results will help you determine which methods work best for your book promotion.

Remember to always consider your budget and align your marketing efforts with your overall goals. What works for one author may not work for another, so it's crucial to adapt your advertising strategies based on your unique circumstances.

CHAPTER 94
After The Book Launch and Beyond

A fter the book launch, there are several important actions and considerations to keep in mind to ensure continued success and maximize the impact of your book. Here are some tips for what to do after the book launch and beyond:

- **Promotional activities:** Continue to promote your book through various channels, such as book signings, author interviews, podcasts, social media, and online advertisements. Use any marketing strategies that have been effective during the launch phase.

- **Engage with readers:** Interact with your readers through social media, book clubs, and author events. This will help to build a community around your book and maintain interest.

- **Gather feedback:** Encourage readers to leave reviews on platforms like Goodreads and Amazon. Feedback can help improve your book and attract more readers.

- **Collaborate with influencers:** Partner with influencers or other authors in your genre to expand your reach and gain new readership.
- **Expand distribution:** Explore other platforms and outlets to distribute your book, such as independent bookstores, libraries, and online retailers.
- **Plan for future projects:** Use the momentum gained from your book launch to plan and prepare for future writing projects. Stay engaged with your audience and consider writing a sequel or exploring related topics.
- **Learn from the process:** Reflect on your book launch and marketing efforts. Reflect on your book launch and marketing efforts to identify what went well and what you can improve upon for future launches.
- **Continue promoting:** Keep promoting your book even after the initial launch phase. Maintain a consistent presence online and through other marketing initiatives.

Remember, building a successful book and author brand takes time and effort. Stay committed, adapt to feedback, and continue to engage with your audience to ensure long-term success beyond the initial launch.

CHAPTER 95
Twenty Places to Sell Your Books

There are many places where you can sell your books, both online and offline. Here are twenty ideas for places to sell your books:

1. **Online marketplaces:** Amazon, eBay, and Etsy are popular platforms where you can list and sell your books.
2. **Your own website:** Create an e-commerce store on your website where readers can purchase your books directly.
3. **Bookstores:** Approach local, independent bookstores and see if they are interested in carrying your book on consignment.
4. **Chain bookstores**: Contact chain bookstores like Barnes & Noble or Books-A-Million to inquire about their consignment or self-published author programs.
5. **Libraries:** Offer copies of your book to local libraries, where they might buy copies or include them in their collection.
6. **Book fairs:** take part in local or regional book fairs where you can sell your books directly to readers.

7. **Literary festivals:** Look for literary festivals or events that showcase authors and their works. These events can provide opportunities to sell your books and connect with readers.

8. **College and university campuses:** Approach campus bookstores or libraries to inquire about selling your books to students, professors, or at book-related events.

9. **Online book clubs:** Seek online book clubs or reading groups that focus on your book's genre. Offer special deals or discounts to members of these groups.

10. **Consignment shops and gift stores:** Approach local gift shops, boutique stores, or consignment shops that may be interested in carrying your book as a unique item for customers.

11. **Coffee shops:** Local coffee shops often have a designated area where they sell books. Inquire about the possibility of featuring your book there.

12. **Local events and farmers' markets:** Set up a booth or table at local events, festivals, or farmers' markets to sell your books directly to attendees.

13. **Community centers and clubs:** Speak with community centers, clubs, or organizations that may be interested in hosting author talks or selling your books during their events.

14. **Non-profit organizations:** Partner with non-profit organizations by donating a portion of book sales to a charity or cause related to your book's theme.

15. **Specialty stores:** Identify specialty stores that align with the topic or theme of your book. For example, if your book is about hiking, approach outdoor gear stores.

16. **Book subscription boxes:** Collaborate with book subscription box services curate themed book packages for

subscribers. Book subscription box services could include your book in their monthly shipments.

17. **Schools and educational institutions:** Speak with school librarians or educators who may be interested in purchasing copies of your book for their classrooms or school libraries.

18. **Workplace libraries:** Approach employers or human resources departments of companies and organizations that have workplace libraries and offer your book.

19. **Online book clubs and author communities:** Engage with online book clubs, forums, and author communities where you can promote your book and connect with potential readers.

20. **Social media platforms:** use social media platforms like Instagram, Facebook, Twitter, or TikTok to promote and sell your books directly to your followers.

Remember, it's essential to research each platform or location and understand their terms, conditions, and potential audience before approaching them to sell your books. Customizing your approach based on your book's genre and audience will help you find the best fit to sell your books.

CHAPTER 96
Carry Your Books with You

A s an author, carrying copies of your books with you at all times can be advantageous for several reasons:

- **Convenience:** Carrying books with you allows you to seize any opportunity to sell your books directly to potential readers. You never know when you might meet someone interested in your genre or eager to support local authors. Having books on hand enables you to make an immediate sale and capitalize on that interest.

- **Impulse purchases:** When someone asks about your work, they may be more likely to make a spontaneous purchase if they can buy a copy on the spot. By carrying books with you, you eliminate the need for potential customers to wait or go through the inconvenience of ordering online or visiting a bookstore.

- **Author events and networking:** Attending author events, conferences, or networking gatherings presents many opportunities to connect with fellow authors, industry professionals, and potential readers. Carrying your books with you allows for immediate exchanges, including book swaps, sales, or promotional giveaways.

- **Personalized signings:** When you carry your books, you're always prepared for impromptu book signings. Whether you find yourself at a local bookstore, a literary event, or even just meeting someone in a casual setting, signing a book personally for a reader creates a memorable and unique experience that can leave a lasting impression.

- **Marketing and visibility:** Displaying your books prominently and sharing them with others wherever you go increases your visibility and acts as a conversation starter. It sparks curiosity, generates interest, and provides opportunities for organic word-of-mouth recommendations as people see your book in public.

- **Marketing collateral:** Books serve as tangible promotional tools. You can give copies to influencers, reviewers, or media professionals who may help spread the word about your work. Having books readily available allows you to include them in press kits, gift bags, or giveaways at events.

- **Flexibility in sales channels:** While online platforms and bookstores are important, carrying your books empowers you to explore additional sales channels. You can sell books at local businesses, pop-up markets, community events, and other venues that may not have formal book-selling arrangements.

Remember, carrying books with you at all times requires some logistical planning and consideration, especially regarding storage, transportation, and organization. Being prepared with a system to handle sales, handling cash or square card readers, and ensuring books are well-protected will help you make the most of these opportunities.

CHAPTER 97
Keep Marketing Your Book

It is key for authors to keep marketing their book for several reasons.

Increase visibility: Continual marketing efforts help generate awareness about the book, making it more visible to potential readers. By consistently promoting the book, authors can reach a wider audience, increasing their chances of attracting new readers.

Build a fan base: Consistent marketing allows authors to nurture and grow their fan base. By engaging with readers and building relationships, authors can cultivate a community of loyal supporters who not only purchase the current book but also expect future releases.

Sustain sales momentum: Marketing efforts help authors maintain a steady flow of sales even after the initial release. By marketing the book consistently, they can sustain interest and encourage ongoing sales, preventing their book from becoming forgotten in a sea of new releases.

Establish credibility: Regular marketing activities, such as guest blogging or speaking engagements, allow authors to show their expertise and build their credibility in their niche. This can lead to increased recognition, more book sales, and potential opportunities for further collaboration or speaking engagements.

Adapt to changing market dynamics: The publishing industry is constantly evolving, and marketing strategies need to adapt accordingly. By consistently analyzing the market, authors can identify new trends, platforms, or promotional opportunities to effectively reach their target audience and stay ahead of the competition.

Overall, keeping up with marketing efforts is essential for authors to maximize the success of their book, connect with readers, and build a sustainable writing career.

CHAPTER 98
Market Your Books Together

If you have more than one book, here are some ways to market them together:

Box sets: Consider packaging your books as a box set or bundle. This can be an effective way to offer readers a discounted value and increase the chances of selling multiple books at once.

Cross-promotion: Promote your other books within each book's front or back matter or offer a discount to readers who purchase both books. This can be an excellent way to encourage readers to check out your other books.

Author's website: showcase all of your books prominently on your author website. You can create dedicated pages for each book, or even a "Books" page that includes information on all of your titles.

Social media: Share updates about your books on your social media accounts, like Facebook, Twitter, Instagram, or LinkedIn. Cross-promote your books by highlighting your other titles in posts and directing followers to your website or retailer pages.

Email newsletter: If you have an email list, use it to promote all of your books. Send regular updates to your subscribers with news about your latest releases, discounts, and promotions.

Book tours: If you're planning a book tour or speaking engagement, promote all of your books during these events. Carry copies of all your books with you on book tours, so readers can purchase them all.

By utilizing some of these strategies, you can effectively market your books together, increase your visibility, and build a bigger audience for your works.

THE FUTURE OF BOOK PUBLISHING

Various changing trends and developments in the industry shape the future of book publishing. One significant trend is the rise of digital publishing. With the increasing popularity of e-books and audiobooks, there is a growing demand for digital content. E-books and audiobooks offer convenience and accessibility, allowing readers to enjoy books in different formats and on various devices.

Another important aspect is self-publishing and independent publishing. With self-publishing platforms and tools, authors now have more control over their works and can publish books without relying solely on traditional publishers. This has opened up opportunities for diverse voices and niche genres to reach readers.

Technology also plays a significant role in the future of book publishing. Artificial intelligence (AI) and machine learning are being employed to analyze data and trends, enabling publishers to make informed decisions about book acquisitions and marketing strategies. Augmented reality (AR) and virtual reality (VR) technology have the potential to enhance the reading experience by incorporating immersive elements.

Personalized content and customization are becoming more prevalent. Publishers are exploring ways to tailor content to individual readers, such as personalized recommendations and interactive storytelling experiences.

It is important to note that the future of book publishing is constantly evolving, and new developments will continue to shape the industry. The impact of emerging technologies, changing reading preferences, and market dynamics will influence the direction book publishing takes in the years to come.

The Impact of Artificial Intelligence (AI) on the Publishing Industry

In recent years, the publishing industry has witnessed a significant transformation because of the emergence of artificial intelligence (AI). Using AI has revolutionized the way publishers create, market, distribute, and analyze books, magazines, and other forms of content. From content creation to personalizing the reader experience, AI has become an essential tool for publishers, authors, and readers alike. This article aims to explore the various ways AI is transforming and enhancing the publishing landscape.

Understanding AI in Publishing

To understand AI in the publishing industry, it is essential to define AI and its significance. AI refers to computer systems that can carry out tasks that usually require human intelligence, such as learning, reasoning, and self-correction. In publishing, AI-powered tools and systems can help with various processes, from predicting market trends to improving the editorial workflow. The potential benefits and opportunities AI brings to publishers, authors, and readers are immense, including enhanced efficiency, personalized content delivery, and improved accessibility.

AI-driven Content Creation and Curation

One of the significant ways AI is changing the publishing industry is through content creation and curation. AI algorithms and natural language processing (NLP) are being used to generate high-quality, personalized content at a faster pace and lower cost. AI-powered tools such as Grammarly and ProWritingAid assist authors with content creation, editing, and proofreading. AI-driven content curation platforms, such as AI2, are enhancing reader engagement by providing personalized recommendations based on reader preferences.

AI-enhanced Editorial Processes

Using AI has also streamlined editorial workflows, such as automated fact-checking and plagiarism detection. Publishers can use AI for analyzing market trends, reader preferences, and predicting successful book genres. However, ethical considerations and challenges associated with AI-driven editorial decision-making need to be addressed to maintain the authenticity and creativity of published works.

AI and Reader Experience

AI-powered recommendation systems personalize reading suggestions based on reader preferences, improving the overall reader experience. AI is also integrated into enhancing accessibility features, such as text-to-speech and language translation. However, concerns about AI's impact on the authenticity and creativity of published works need to be acknowledged and addressed.

Future Implications and Challenges

The future implications of AI in the publishing industry are vast, with emerging AI technologies already entering the market.

However, concerns about job displacement and the role of human creativity in an AI-driven publishing landscape need to be addressed. Ethical guidelines and responsible implementation of AI in the industry are crucial to ensure the long-term success of AI integration.

AI has the potential to transform and enhance the publishing industry in various ways. As AI continues to develop, publishers, authors, and readers will benefit from the advancements and improvements it brings. The responsible use of AI, combined with human creativity, can lead to greater access to information, increased engagement, and a more efficient publishing process. It is up to the industry to embrace AI while keeping ethical considerations at the forefront.

ABOUT THE AUTHOR

Author and publisher Ann Aubitz has worked in the printing and publishing business for over thirty years. She has worked for some of the largest printers in the world and now works as a publisher for her own publishing company.

As a publisher, Ann wants to pull back the curtain on the publishing process. From manuscript, editing, design, printing, and marketing, publishing a book is a complex journey. But it doesn't have to feel overwhelming. With the proper guidance, you can navigate the path successfully.

Bringing your book to life is an exciting process. As someone who has been through it many times, she is happy to share insights into transforming your manuscript into a published book. The journey involves dedication, but is rewarding. She looks forward to helping you achieve your book publishing dreams.

Contact Information

Kirk House Publishers
1250 East 115th Street, Burnsville MN 55337
612-781-2815
ann@kirkhousepublishers.com
kirkhousepublishers.com